Ready: What to Expect when Starting c
wants to start a business. This no-
cal tools integrated with the social/emotional realities of starting or
running a biz. As a business owner, I know this would have been
helpful to me when I started out. Lyndsey brings a wonderful mix of
intelligence from her MBA with her experience from opening House
of Steep. The areas of fear, relationships, and intuition are particularly
interesting to me, because these topics usually do not come up in biz
books, and they are extremely relevant. I'm delighted to have this book
to give to clients and friends who want to start a business in the future!

—Pleasance Silicki, author of
Delight: Eight Principles for Living with Joy And Ease
and founder of lil omm yoga and LOLA community

Ready: What to Expect when Starting a Business, by Lyndsey Clutteur
DePalma, is beautifully written, with a style and tone that is nurturing, pragmatic, and quite compelling. She is extremely honest about
the journey of business ownership/entrepreneurship and does not leave
the readers with preconceived notions of what it will take to prepare,
launch, and run a business. She fully exposes herself—her excitement,
the fears, her missteps, the most challenging and proudest moments—
to help future business owners understand all of the ramifications,
consequences, and possible rewards of taking on this entrepreneurial
challenge. It's a refreshing read. Her insights are both humbling and
empowering; and it will emotionally, mentally, and financially prepare
those who want to launch and grow a business that both supports
their lifestyle goals and fulfills their purpose.

—Mali Phonpadith, CEO, SOAR Community Network,
TEDx speaker, #1 international bestselling author,
OWN Belief Team partner

Ready: What to Expect When Starting a Business
by Lyndsey Clutteur DePalma

published by
Liveliest Press
6312 Seven Corners Center #144
Falls Church, Virginia 22044
www.liveliestpress.com

ISBN: 978-1-7332584-0-1 trade paperback
       978-1-7332584-1-8 electronic book

Design and composition: www.dmargulis.com

First printing

MANUFACTURED IN THE UNITED STATES OF AMERICA

To Nick

. . . and your willingness to come along for the ride

Contents

Ready

Introduction

$\mathcal{S}$tarting a business is like giving birth. To do it right you'll need time to prepare, you'll experience pain thresholds unimaginable, and you'll have to call deep on your resources—your own when you're lying awake at 3 a.m., and your support network when the going gets tougher. Be it the level of effort required or how fragile a business can be in its infancy, strong parallels exist between the birthing of concepts or humans. For me, starting a business was my destiny. Even though my first business journey took me along a winding path of marvel and mayhem to a place where I was serving tea in my cafe with my firstborn (human) strapped to my chest because the scheduled server was out sick, the path to that place felt right. Hard at times, but right. And in that life-will-be-changing-forevermore-starting-to-morrow moment once my business plan was complete, I still managed to find peace in this new crossroads of life, thanks entirely to my genes. My mom owned a small retail business and my grandma started a travel business. *Finding a way* is in my DNA. Still, it wasn't until I was approaching the age of thirty and studying to get my MBA that I realized I wanted nothing less than to start something in the name of something meaningful like my foremothers did, something called my *purpose*. And while my original intention of earning an MBA was to become savvier in the corporate world, what I actually left with was a burning desire to create something new and the confidence that I could figure it out.

The moment I created the space to uncover my purpose, it broke into my consciousness with undeniable clarity. I'd been tossing around the concept of a tea house that connected patrons with natural health and relaxation through herbs and self-awareness for a while, but owning my own shop wasn't a priority. It was one of several concepts that I thought about starting someday. In fact, at the time I was only contemplating my *why*: I'd been lucky enough to stumble into some corporate roles that offered career growth, but if I was going to be purposeful with my working days, I needed to maximize my opportunities. That's why I enrolled in part-time MBA school in the first place: to enhance my skills and broaden my thinking. There's nothing enchanting about layering a graduate program on top of your fifty-hour work week, but it felt right, and it made space for what was to come.

The funny thing is, once I learned how other businesses had found *their* way, my tea house concept made perfect sense. Understanding business ownership through various case studies is what helped bring into sharper view my vision. And where chance favors the prepared, I had incredible MBA peers willing to help me test my model and cheer me on. My idea aligned in my heart and on paper, and others validated it. The timing seemed right from a competition and demand perspective. For the rest (I was aware there would be surprises), I reasoned my grit and genetic makeup would complement any learning opportunity that was missed in the planning. The great abyss of missing business lessons that did ensue became the making of this book, because an education doesn't buy that many shortcuts, not in real life. This book aims to be the bridge between what you can learn from business school (and the internet) and the thrilling, gut-wrenching, redefining-the-word-*difficult* reality that is entrepreneurship. As I said, starting a business is like giving birth. I want to tell the story that would have saved me so much time, money, and emotional energy. I can't reclaim any of it, but I can still regard it as hard-earned, beautiful lessons.

The stories in this book are the equivalent of my mom-to-be diary, or the connections I drew from my own experience and the examples I studied in business school. They chronicle my learnings from my encounters with startups and, as any journal would be, they're both revealing and cringe-worthy. My journaling goal was simply to record my experiences. There were highs I wanted to remember to tell my one-day grandkids about and lows I couldn't tell anyone about. There were many surprises that I wished someone had told me about, so I could have done things differently. Perhaps the biggest one is that not many other business owners share intimate details about their own surprises. I was struck by the contrast between how lovely the idea of business ownership sounded and how complex the reality was. In much the same way that people don't talk about the scary or grisly stuff when having a real baby, people also don't talk about the dark stuff when a living brand is on the line. Perhaps silence prevails because the experience of birthing (both human and business) is so personal, and because we've had centuries of conditioning telling us to "be strong" and not show any rawness or vulnerability. Or maybe just because we don't want to scare anyone away, but in my experience, most people have a mixture of easy, natural flow, and hard-learned lessons. The gap is between those who are willing to first recognize those highs and lows and willing to talk about it . . . and those who are not. And part of the reason for not talking about it is that starting a business takes up an astonishing amount of time and energy. Most of us simply don't have the time to stop and talk about it.

I did have time. I left my corporate job too early with a "how hard can it be?" attitude when I was admittedly surprised to find out my concept had legs. I was then doubly surprised to find myself in a cavernous space between "it could work!" and actually making it happen. I figured if I was learning so much, other business "moms" pregnant with their own concepts could benefit from my notes. But surprises or not, business books can't possibly prescribe the path to success because every business is different. . . and besides, aren't we doing this because we want to light up our own path, our own purpose? This is a delicate dance, especially for traditional business books. So my "if only I had known" has become the tale of "let me share some stories." They are not meant to tell you what to do but rather how to approach the beautiful and sometimes scary moments of starting something of your own. I shed light on how lovingly deep the experience can be, the high highs, and the "why didn't this come up in birthing class?!" lows. Many parents look back and say they wouldn't change a thing, or that they didn't know what they were missing until they had a kid; the same love stories emerge in business. I am a firm believer that sometimes business is just business and that your business is not *you*. But I also recognize that there's always a person behind the business, and as sterile or impersonal as it can sometimes feel you have to be, the inherent humanity cannot be denied. Amidst the day-to-day blocking and tackling and check-listing, you're holding up something so much bigger than you. I, and so many of my peers, didn't realize how much *nurturing* goes into going solo or taking on an enterprise that more directly ties efforts to rewards (versus an organization who may pay you a fraction of what they bill your services at), or how sleepless those early nights are. And I didn't realize how right-on my observations were about the process of birthing a business until I had a human baby. Indeed, the anticipation, the waiting, the lessons in patience, resilience, and humbleness resonate to the core. Birthing a concept is simply a gorgeous feeling: one of the hardest and yet most sensational endeavors of my life. And so, with this book, a new creation is born, one that helps light the path for other entrepreneurs.

Ready: What to Expect when Starting a Business is for the hopeful "parent" who is starting a new business, building their brand from scratch, or who needs some sister-tribe advice and examples to help them get more comfortable with what lies ahead. This book is part business know-how and part spiritual awareness guide. I share my experiences in building a concept from mere thought to a unique retail/relaxation tea shop, along with anecdotes from my peers and clients. The stories lead into recommendations for tools to help you take your learning to the next level as you choose to grow in one area or another. Ultimately, you get to figure this out for yourself, and I encourage you to do just that, using these stories as examples and suggestions to help you realize that the answer is within reach. Even though there will be days when all you want is for someone to tell you the right answer, finding your own answers is what makes you an entrepreneur, and no book can do that for you.

Refer to this book for a little bit of wisdom and a lot of reassurance that you're on the right track for a high-caliber business that is aligned with the instincts that brought you to this point. This book (and its sequels) will also help the "mom"-preneur who is ready to grow her business to the next level but wants to reconnect with the basics first. Reconnecting to why you're here and how you launched will help restore your sense of inspiration and purpose, fortify roots that help you grow, and recognize the sometimes-overlooked goodness that's keeping you upright.

You'll get the most out of the stories and advice in this book if you already have a concept in mind. While plenty of clients come to me saying they know they want to have their own business but haven't clarified the concept, those that benefit the most know their *why* and understand the special sauce of what their company will offer the world. But even if you're not there yet, hearing how others have navigated will help. You'll be able to think more clearly about your own *why*, what your highs and lows may look like, and you'll ultimately deepen your connection with your business flow. This "closeness to flow" is something that men and women can both experience, but our feminine energy allows us to nurture deeply this Universal energy in a way that ends up fueling us faster, farther, and deeper in the business world. Thanks to our divine ability to bring life to this earth, we are naturally equipped to tune into our instincts and understand the tests, the beauty, and the evolution in a way that more masculine-driven energies are often not. It's our gift, it is awesome, and we celebrate the many women who are following their purpose and tapping into their innate talents to create across the world.

It's not only about following a passion and discovering a deeper connection to the rewards by default. It's the authentic voice we're able to extend to our customers and in turn the enrichment of experience they feel from engaging with us and our fire; it's the circle of life that each of us seeks as social animals and in doing what vividly matters in our lifetime.

But like most relationships and experiences that enliven us or allow us to evolve, the chance for love and care comes with the risk of disappointment, even resentment. This entrepreneurial paradox (e-paradox as I refer to it) is a topic I introduce in this book. Specifically, it refers to what happens when an entrepreneur wants something badly and loves it dearly, but because of these strong feelings, that same object of desire (a goal, a financial milestone, etc.) can become deeply frustrating in the space of a moment. I experienced this when I fell out of flow with my retail business. The tea shop I founded was a gorgeous extension of me and offered relaxation and access to natural health (tea, herbs, essential oils, healthy bites, and reflexology) in a busy and desirable area of Arlington, Virginia. I loved my business and the joy it brought me to be able to provide peace in such a fast-paced area. Flow was natural and I knew I was living my purpose, but when things were hard—staff quitting, customers complaining, logistics competing with scalability, and usually all on the same day—I felt flooded. Sometimes I didn't *like* the thing I *loved*.

This paradox is natural in relationships. Deep feelings can swiftly reverse when one is operating at such a high velocity and sensory level. It's important to note how much time you spend feeling disdain, versus the time you spend enamored with your work. You remind yourself that low feelings are temporary, you focus on the good, and you stick around, hoping the sweet lingers longer than the bitter because you love this thing. But that dogged determination to focus on the positive can sometimes mask the signals your subconscious is sending you, lowering your tolerance for the day-to-day stressors, until suddenly you find yourself broken and burned out, with nothing left but an attachment to the good parts and zero reserves to carry it further.

Take my mom's retail business. She bought an existing business that was doing well but was in a location that wasn't ideal. She also took over before the big box retailers moved into town, so her flow really only lasted for the first two years of business. After that, it was brutal. She needed to move but couldn't afford the rent of a more competitive location (thanks to the new chains increasing the demand). She needed to innovate and become relevant to the customer of tomorrow, but her business model catered to small-towners who were retiring and not spending money the same way as when her predecessor was in charge. Times got tough and she poured her savings into the business. Her employees stole from her, and even though it was a constant back-breaker for the decade she remained open, she *still* looks back on the experience fondly because of those first couple of glory years. This distortion is a prime example of the e-paradox, and it's worth paying attention to, because things will not go as planned. Your commitment to your new creation will test you and evolve you, as anything truly worth doing should. Keep this concept in the back of your mind, even during times of appreciation and joy, while ebbing and flowing with your business.

Just as there are times for your business to champion through, there are also moments when even the fearless captain must take a break. Women are natural warriors, it's true. But we're also nurturers, and anyone in touch with their feminine expression needs to honor this in order to sustain. We'll see examples of how this can look while you're smack in the middle of everything you're responsible for and all those things that only *you* know how to handle. As we address the basic elements of building a business (marketing, finance, etc.), we will examine the times it calls for a yang-like energy (action-oriented, driven, or productive) and when it calls for yin. Still, this is *your* business, so *you* get to decide whether you show up as warrior or nurturer, depending on what the forecast calls for. And speaking of climate, even the more aggressive, testosterone-led women can still become weathered by business. It's important to consider the dichotomies of character the business is asking for and to respond in the best way.

One question that comes up for many women is whether or not they have the (ahem) *male parts* to succeed in a masculine-energy arena like business. The answer is a resounding *yes!* Quitting your job to fulfill your purpose can be the scariest and most eulogy-worthy thing you may ever do. But you have to do it right. There are questions to ask yourself first, such as Can I afford to not have this job? Am I having the impact or other fulfillment that could keep me going if I never launch my own business? Am I still learning and growing? Am I having fun? The answers may outweigh the fear and thus give you peace of mind. It may be that it's a matter of *when* versus *if.* And if you're still committed but can't work out the timing, the great news is that for most concepts, plenty of startup tasks can be done in your free time while keeping your day job. Let's face it: money can bring peace if it's helping you fund your dream. For that reason alone, making as much money as you can in the early "trimesters" is highly encouraged. Timing your day job exit must be a part of your flow and harmony. And once you've given your exit timing some loving thought, go ahead and put that goal on the calendar. The business world stands to benefit from even more feminine influence, and we're seeing that across corporations today with the "pink economy," where businesses are valuing more social skills like empathy, intuition, and care. It's an exciting time to birth a business!

If you're still having doubts about whether you're cut out for the job, consider this quick list.

You shouldn't be an entrepreneur if

▶ at any point in your prior job you felt like there was too much work to do, or the work didn't suit your preferences. Starting your own business means work and not all of it is strategic or sexy.

▶ vacationing and escaping reality is your only way to live. Business ownership can often mean no extended time off, possibly for years.

▶ you have a hard time finishing what you start. If you're entrepreneurial-spirited, you'll likely have another idea in the not-so-distant future. So, can you see yourself committed to *this* thing for the next three to ten years? If you can't, then you may have what many in the industry call "professional ADD." I wouldn't recommend entrepreneurship at this stage in your personal evolution. It's a marathon that requires stamina and emotional fortitude.

▶ you're uncomfortable with the unknown or don't have an appetite for low lows. You have to be strong enough to handle discomfort and uncertainty. Crystal balls and perfect scripts do not exist; honing the art of seeing life as one big lesson is a skill that entrepreneurs practice.

▶ you want to get rich quick. If that's where you're at, then starting a business will require your sharp redefinition of success.

Most entrepreneurs joke that their business was an overnight success that took five years (sometimes ten!).

▶ you prefer strategy to execution. Said differently, if you are the ideas gal but not the doer, you may feel more fulfilled in an environment that rewards you for riffing. Staying in love with a concept without loving the *how* can challenge your motivation in the early days. Read *The E-Myth* or *The E-Myth Revisited* to understand how people generally aren't equipped for *all the hats* of entrepreneurship.

And if you're still not sure, I invite you to read on. As you read the stories within this book, you'll gain a clearer sense of whether this is a journey you want to take. Chances are, once your financials are promising and you can imagine in detail how a business may work for you, you'll become more passionate about your path.

How to Use This Book

The goal is readiness. Secondary to my sitting with you and talking through your big dreams and your tactical execution, the ability to get your mind, stomach, ego, and punch list on the same party boat comes down to two things: confidence and aptitude. This will come in the form of anecdotes, business parallels for practical application, and practice, where at the end of each chapter you can marinate the theories and see how that chapter applies to your business dream.

In this book, I use terms normally associated with actual pregnancy. Rather than putting them in quotes every time, which would be tiresome for both of us, let's set some ground rules right up front. When I use words like "expecting," "birthing," or "parenthood," I am referring to the process of anticipating, creating, or growing your business, unless otherwise noted. "Go bag" is your curated collection of your necessities to get. it. done. If it seems too literal, it is meant to be a joke. "Diapers" and "blowouts" are generally associated with the less than ideal aspects of parenting, if you haven't yet come upon those terms in real life to be able to appreciate what I'm getting at. We can take life really seriously sometimes, so where there is a joke to be had, why not roll with it? No actual baby manual will have a step-by-step guide and neither will this, although it does have timelines to consider, since so much hinges on timing. There are no right answers, only right choices for given moments. Through examples of other business parents sharing their experiences and wisdom, my hope is to make those choices seem less daunting. This book offers you shortcuts to solving many new-business-mom surprises, stories to learn what not to do, and best of all, a platform to help you learn to trust your instincts in a new environment. We don't seem to be wired to phone in something as monumental as conception and nurturing a being, so alongside our can-do attitude, seeking wisdom to make sure we're doing what's best for baby is also important. Lastly, there will be opportunities to reflect on the stories and ways to offer your own creation some relative love via the exercises and artistic expressions at the end of each chapter.

Most business parents "only" do this a few times, so take comfort that you're neither the first nor the last newbie to seek knowledge and understanding in bringing something beautiful to life. If this is your first foray into the startup world, you can take heart that even second-timers refer back to their notes at the end of each chapter because the blur from sleep deprivation or pleasure has masked all memory of the pain.

With or without a manual, a coach, or a partner, this can be one of the most terrifying yet fulfilling things you'll ever do. You'll be outside of your comfort zone, confronting your fears, embracing your strengths, and experiencing the spectrum of emotions, fueled by endorphins and rewards in unexpected shapes and sizes. The work will be like you've never experienced before, because it's all *yours*. The excitement will be beautiful. Business parenthood will be humbling.

It will surprise you. You'll tell yourself a hundred times that you're here for the evolution and not necessarily the answers. You'll feel like you're alone, but after reading this book, you'll know that you're not. And from one business mom to another, I know that you will be great.

Part I

The Joys and Jolts
of Having a Baby Business

1

What to Expect in the Early Moments

So you're having a business! The excitement, the anticipation, the fears, *the responsibility* . . . all of the feelings you might expect while creating a real-life baby, sans the diapers. This is a time of high velocity and extreme emotion, and preparing yourself physically, emotionally, and tactically will ready you for what lies ahead. Your instincts are kicking in. *Something big is about to happen!* There's a reason entrepreneurs joke about their business as their baby. You will develop an intense bond with it. Having a business makes you feel full—of purpose and also of doubt, within the same 30 seconds. And like a real baby, the endless demands bring deeper joy and an equally profound sense of fulfillment. You are the sole person who knows how to love it best, because it was *your* concept and no one else is better suited for the job . . . yet.

It was this strong pull to create that got me through every detail of my business plan. It was the kinetic energy that carried me over each hurdle. And even if my future self could have revealed how *difficult* it is to love something so *hard* and so long, it wouldn't have deterred me. Creation is a force. It's nearly impossible to scratch the itch when an "it" idea comes that still makes sense after the number crunching and soul searching. And standing back and regarding your idea on paper is a driver that validates your instincts. Validation is an even bigger force. *And it was good . . .* most of the time.

That's exactly how it went. I followed my heart and my business plan and had an incredible time developing, birthing, and nurturing my business. The same way that a positive pregnancy test foreshadows the numerous tests that follow, identifying a need and a solution (the business to be) sets us down a path of evolution. Even with all the setbacks and hard work (much harder than I imagined), it was still my life's *why*, lessons and all. Yet anytime I was asked "What's new?" I found myself unable to speak of such epiphanies. I knew it was right and I loved how I felt with this concept growing inside me, but I also knew it wasn't time to share the news. Too much shifting in my mind, body, and soul. Too much to figure out before my ego would allow inviting others into my new world. Too much fear to recognize and work through. Eventually I would, but not before some significant shifts.

Expect Silence

I didn't set out to achieve this stillness when my business journey commenced in 2010. The emotional pull was already there, and I knew there was more to my walk on this planet than a corporate job would offer. My work was satisfying, but it was not enough. I wanted to do something bold and self-fulfilling. I didn't need a pat on the back and a raise. I needed tangible results and to make a difference in a busy community by providing something that reminded everyone to take it easy, to take back a piece of themselves, and to focus on natural health. I wanted to make tea the indulgence that coffee had become, and with all of this intention and desire, my first baby business was conceived. Still, with no prior experience, truly vetted business plan, or business partner to bolster confidence, I retreated to the safety of silence until it felt right to share my plans.

This silence is important because reality is setting in. You're still assessing your goals and how they will manifest. Receiving feedback is important, but that will come later. Centering on what your instincts are telling you is more critical in this early phase: *What does this mean for me, my family, my finances, my social life (and more) if this concept comes to life? What if I am the only one interested in this offering? What am I missing? Does any of this matter since I have my "it" idea? No! But what if it does?* This is a lot to process. It may make sense to take time before inviting the thoughts or feelings of others. Plus a lot can change in the embryonic stage, so best to play it safe for now and enjoy your fun secret a little longer.

Silence buys you openness. Keeping the secret while you mentally work through some things can portend the future. Nearly every decision for your business will come with some level *Application to Business* of quiet reflection on whether it's the right decision. Sure, you will have sounding boards, but you don't want to sound the alarm every time a question comes up. For some new moms, each bump, scratch, sneeze, and cough is reason to ask her friends and family for advice. There's also an unfolding of privacy in business that is innate and fans freely only in time. The instinct to prove we can figure it out kicks in early, but feeling confident that we are one with the whole experience, are resolved, and can confidently handle it shows up about halfway into the voyage. And when it all comes together in your mind, there is an inclination to quietly reflect, to process these feelings and new instincts, to call on your inner warrior to make sense of everything new and raw. *And embrace it all.* Your impulses are letting you practice what it means to be open to life, born in this concept you're gifting to the world.

Those motherly instincts, even with the firstborn, are usually right. Still, sharpening skills and readiness is something we all like to do, and with some guidance, new moms can be right *and* successful. They get to learn what it means to be a true hero, fulfilling their natural talents while nurturing something that is bigger than them. And here you are, sweet mama-to-be, embarking on what will arguably be the most eye-opening, meaningful, and defining period of your life. Plenty of entrepreneurs see this period differently and broadcast their plans immediately, and I respect that. But whichever way is chosen, you won't find an entrepreneur who regrets bringing their concept to life. The lessons are in both approaches, with the one who is open to the lessons as the one enjoying the ride.

Expect Uncertainty

Someone once said that the experience of parenthood is realizing how little you know. And as a first-time business parent, trying to prove to the world of raised eyebrows that inexperience + wild concept = success, I can attest to the daily reminder of how uncertain this world can be. I didn't believe that I needed, nor could I afford, a business coach to help me out of my head and into action. I'd save the coaching for when I needed to be strategic with the piles of money I was about to make, rather than discuss the nuance of every. single. choice. As a result, many a precious hour was spent ruminating on the right decision, which not only wasted time but also generated a recurring, recognized, and disconnected feeling: so much to think about, not a lot of answers or guidance. Sure, I would casually mention to my spouse and my closest confidantes an idea I was noodling, but I didn't have anyone who could truly understand my challenges, because few people knew about my endeavors. Plus I didn't want to come across as completely incompetent before even leaving the gates. Still, thinking first and sharing later felt right. Nevertheless, it's lonely in that entrepreneurial head, and scary too. Not knowing what manner of lesson is next doesn't help in getting through the first batch of lessons. And thinking positively about the future, while evolutionarily necessary, can sometimes feel like you're lying to yourself in the wake of having to learn *every. damn. thing.*

This lonesome feeling was not discussed in business school. No one told me about how often I would need to get out of my head and assure myself that if so many other business moms and dads—roughly twenty-seven million entrepreneurs in the United States alone—figured it out, I could too. But the lows were real. As were the highs. Just as the body biologically begins to respond with the knowledge of being "with baby," so too does the mind begin to adjust to being "with business." For me, the excitement that came from connecting my work efforts directly with financial compensation, working autonomously, managing my own time, being brave enough to take such serious risks, and finally fulfilling my purpose is what fueled my enjoyment of the highs. But yet again, I kept things private. While this feeling was easier to share with others, I might not have done it enough because of the fears. One way to let those feelings be what they need to be and to normalize all the highs and lows is to journal them. Even if you can't talk to someone, at least you're honoring those feelings, and that will help you get on with what is to come. And ideally those feelings become just that and don't pose any sort of distraction from your mission. No one is saying you can't share with others what's coming up, but in the unpredictability, and while it's raw and new, there is a gorgeous awakening to what is happening. It's worth the quiet for you to get comfortable. Let the uncertainty be the teacher of presence and attunement that it is.

Uncertainty begets confidence. The relationship to the self strengthens through exercises in ego checks, patience, grace, and acceptance; and commitment and resilience emerge. I

Application to Business

thought I was patient, but feelings expressed in isolation revealed that I might be a little more controlling than I realized when mama instincts were kicking in. I thought I was persuasive, but when potential partners weren't budging on negotiations, doubt over my negotiation skills—me—set in, and suddenly, perhaps, I'm not as persuasive as I thought. Yet that was one of a zillion moments where I had to recognize the fear and choose to let it teach me something. Instead of denying it and feeling defeated, I allowed it to teach me to go deeper on what really mattered. In the negotiations example, I was usually able to get to a comfortable place if I picked myself up one more time and asked differently. Persistence and connecting with what I needed were the vehicles, with confidence being the beautiful byproduct. And it went on. Learning to welcome doubt and fear was my teacher for my preparation for being the most confident and grounded business mom I could be. Releasing control mattered, because my timeline was not as relevant as the lessons I learned over and over and over and over again, lessons that helped me get comfortable with my new skin that bore a glow of expectation. Recognizing negative self-talk and my ability to choose which stories to see as true or limiting only came about because of the perspective I achieved from having done this scary thing, embraced the fear and its wisdom, and detached from the moment to see the situation from a distance. This clarity of what was going on—otherwise known as my relationship to myself, otherwise known as mastery of mindset, otherwise known as confidence in the making—supported my business tenfold. It was important to hone this early on otherwise those emotions would have stood in my way; in recognizing them, I was able to manage them. And therefore manage my business, even when the scope of my effort was simply sketching plans, making a sustainable business model, and being okay with my gaps in experience.

To recap, because this is important, step 1 is accepting that uncertainty is armoring you with confidence, and step 2 is recognizing your alignment with your innate compass. If it didn't matter to you, it

> *If it didn't matter to you, it wouldn't be scary.*

wouldn't be scary. This is the calibration that only happens when you go down an unknown path or do something in the name of purpose. You get to connect with your internal guide! When you're downtrodden because What *is* the best decision here? remember that a template or how-to manual won't get you to this depth of experience, and even if you had one, it wouldn't allow you to stand out as a business. Even with an MBA, you wouldn't know *how*, you'd only learn *theories* to better learn on the job. Once you accept that *you* have what it takes to figure out what's right for *you* and *your* business, it's easy to point in the direction of marketing goals, strategic planning, or other tactical resourcing. And that's where this book meets you: a hint of reminding you of your path; a dash of this-is-how-you-can, sister; mom wisdom; and a pinch of you-will-be-fine assertions, since you at least don't have to learn *my* lessons the hard way. Trust that you're capable of loving this concept the best. And by picking up this book you can supplement your newfound confidence with some tips and best practices from business parents who came before you.

Expect Financial Shifts

Once upon a time, I loved to shop. I'd shop on my lunch break, I'd shop when I had friends in town, I'd shop for a meeting or event. Then I decided to throw all kinds of money at a dream, and my love of shopping vanished. Why? Fear. There are fears we can acknowledge and then move on from. Then there are verified, holy cow, what-does-this-mean fears that can paralyze you. They almost always translate to *my bank account can't stomach this.* Babies cost money. Lots of it. The obvious projections (diapers, clothing, safety) are the tip of the iceberg, and anything purchased will either have an unpredictable shelf life or require some sort of proprietary refill. Because you don't know what to expect, any perceived illness has you hauling into the doctor's office with an abundance of caution. Those same rackets and ratcheting costs happen also in the business world. Even if you're tiptoeing into the world of business birthing by part-timing your concept or phasing its launch, there will be up-front costs, surprise costs, and *I should write a book about all the costs* costs. You may already have a plan to address the financial aspects of your endeavor, but let me take a moment to talk about the reality. Either directly or indirectly, your relationship with finances will change. Domestically, I managed the finances and purchases because discussions around the "meals and entertainment" category on our family balance sheet was a polarizing topic for my husband and me. Besides, being the one to get things done (i.e., paying the bills) meant that household comptroller was a role I assumed, only to realize that simply paying the bills and making sure we had enough money for a few goals didn't make me a good CFO. A good CFO looks hard at the goal first and makes sure short- and long-term investments are in *constant* alignment. But an evolutionary shift was afoot. The old me would say, *that's okay, I'll make sure we spend less next month.* The new me was seeing the savings account as the *only* source of initial funds for my project, so every single penny spent was under scrutiny because it was the only money I could count on. The shift of my relationship to finances had already begun simply because building a business was so much more rewarding than spending money. At about the same time, my perhaps omniscient cat dumped water over my only business asset (my computer), furthering my fear of unknown financial status. Preparing for unknown/unexpected costs became more important than previous luxuries, and many domestic decisions were secretly weighed against my six-month business forecast because my savings were surreptitiously allocated for funding ideas in the business. This, of course, was unsavory to my relationships. Even for moms lucky enough to avoid leveraging their own savings, there is still the mental impact of *that unknown* that makes spending so much more complex.

Everyone hopes for the best and believes in their forecasts or projections, but you really can't predict your take-home so you won't know what you can afford, vacations and holiday spending included. It will probably feel natural because . . . baby! Even the most solid business concepts endure dry spells, so bootstrapping and being smart with all sources of money is prudent until you understand the complete needs of your business.

Savvy CFO. No matter what your trade is, if you're in business, you're in the business of making money. It does you no service to pretend that the finances take care of themselves. *Application to Business* And while still in the early stages, it's helpful to understand how much you should plan to savor the topic of money. How much money is needed for you to keep doing the thing that fills your love bucket, reverberates to the world, and can make a difference? That's a healthy focus on money and it is funding your dream.

When starting out, I heard that things will cost three times as much as I thought. Well, timelines usually need a multiplier of three as well. If you hope that you can hire a freelance web designer for $1,000, multiply that by three. Even if you can find someone for that amount, add in hosting fees, privacy fees, added security fees, figuring-out-what-you-really-want-after-the-site-has-been-up-for-a-while fees, and in just your first year, you will have overspent your original estimates. I promise. Telling you this isn't meant to add to your fears, but if anything keeps you up at night, it will be fear, and finances can occupy a large part of the fearful mind. The only way through fear is *through*, and soon you'll be savvier about not how you spend it but how you value that gorgeous, wonderful, incredible dollar.

The good news is that your transition to your new life involves getting smart and comfortable with possibility. Not only can possibility fuel desires, when the numbers make sense on paper, most budding parents can relax about financial fears and shift to others. With sound numbers, it can work out. I've dedicated my time to writing a book about the things not many other business moms talk about publicly, so hear this: Plan for the worst, but dream up and set your intention on the best! Still dream up and plan to take that vacation. Maybe not in the same quarter that you made another big investment, but definitely act as if you're making space for something rewarding that comes from calculated decisions. Even if you're still in the creative conception stage, it's mental heavy lifting and you need to reward yourself . . . occasionally. Plan carefully, save well, pace smartly, and your savings and your sanity will thank you.

In planning for the worst, consider your financial assumptions around the biggest fears you have. This will absolutely help you when it's time to recognize whether the fear is a speed bump or a mountain that requires recalculation. Your specific fear list might be different, but here are a few expectations that could help your overall peace if you think them through and embrace *planning for the worst* so you can use your energy *hoping for the best.*

All in all, fear around financials (be it personal or to fund your plans) will be a force multiplier: You're losing predictable income, you're dipping into your savings, and you're unlikely to make money right away. Be okay with this. It's not fun to embrace financial worst-case scenarios, but this can make or break you early on, so it's worth the attention. Bootstrapping can look like anything from paying for talent in equity to bartering services to deferred payment arrangements. You have options, so don't feel completely strapped. Through doing these exercises, and even through honoring money for what it buys for your dream, your financial health will improve.

---

*Plan carefully, save well, pace smartly,
and your savings and your sanity will thank you.*

I was excited to tell my husband about my business idea. He knew how unfulfilled I was at work and I thought he would appreciate my strategy to use my graduate degree. I had sketched my plans in detail and left no room for question, or so I believed. The relaxation tea house was a perfect business concept that the world would love! Except, I had no access to investors, my savings were largely tied up in an IRA, the concept was weighty, and I would need to hire staff as soon as practically possible . . . putting a $100,000 price tag on the business before it would be up and running. Plus we would lose my income for a period of time.

I'd rehearsed my pitch to my husband, a lawyer good at finding flaws in arguments. I envisioned what he might say: *Do you have a business plan? Are you out of your mind?* And I'd prepared pie charts and pro forma reports to address his concerns.

My pitch did not go well. "You want to do *what* with our home equity?" "You want to put off having a family for who knows how much longer?" "You want to sell *what* and expect a *return* on the investment?" His look of bewilderment was probably the most surprising. I took it personally. I dug in and kept putting graphs and projections in front of him (thankfully I had already created a business plan to help back my theories). Why, and mostly how, were already there, but I needed about six more of these difficult conversations before I could articulate precisely how it could be pulled off. And six more long and painful discussions before he would realize how important this was to me, that it wasn't going away easily, and that if I didn't go for it, I'd always wonder. He eventually and reluctantly agreed to *consider* it. I was already emotionally attached to this concept(ion) and unable to appreciate the practicalities of his resistance. I was crestfallen. Even my biggest cheerleaders (my spouse and my mom) weren't as enthusiastic about the idea as I was. They did not recognize my "it" idea as genius. Turns out, they had some valid points and there was more

Financial Readiness
through Expectation Management

Expectation	Reality	Advice
I will start making money in two months.	Maybe, but unlikely unless you have clients who have already signed contracts.	Ensure you have two to three months' savings to cover this lull (minimum estimate pending risk tolerance and strength of your backup plan).
I will save so much money in old job costs	True! You probably won't have to commute/park and might not reward yourself with a mocha every day. You won't have to refresh your wardrobe, and you get to deduct so much on taxes. Networking coffees will still come up, but on the whole, this reality is a positive one (factoring out the whole salary loss bit).	Plan for that "coffee" money to be put to good use elsewhere :)
I will quit my job and open with a retail location in three to six months.	Plan for up to eighteen months, because location, location, location (and a few broker lessons learned— see appendix for retail space lessons).	It can take more than three months to negotiate a lease. Time is money, so keep an income stream as long as you can.
Bankers are going to give me a loan, so I won't need savings.	Bankers want to see you have an easy way to repay their loan, assuming they love your concept and can still collateralize your home and car. And SBA loans are often prohibitively expensive and not startup friendly.	Keep your day job or a side hustle as long as you possibly can, perhaps even after launching at a reduced schedule, to float your operations until you know your seasonality.
I can build my own website to save money.	You can, but it depends on how much of your brand relies on the site. Experts say to outsource what you aren't an expert in, but when you're getting started with limited resources, that's not possible. Some corners shouldn't be cut if what your customers will see is your site (not you via a service or experience to earn or deepen their trust).	Don't assume you can do everything yourself, and try to budget accordingly. Your time is precious, and websites are complex and important. A self-designed splash page or basic layout that's crisp but bootstrapped can help your cash flow go further if your concept allows.

Expectation	Reality	Advice
I need to build my savings and keep working, so I'll outsource what I don't have time for.	This is contrary to the above assumption, but the point here is balance between figuring it out to save money and hiring out what you don't have time for. Outsourcing can get expensive, and sometimes you need to try it first to discover your true limitations. Some outsourced experts are necessary and some are a luxury. You have to figure out if the trade-off is to hire it out in order to keep earning a salary to fund your dream.	Even if you're still working, ask yourself if this is a function you truly don't have time for, then consider if there's an exchange/barter available. Figure out what you have to offer to possibly help build a colleague or other business owner's portfolio. Check your friends' skillsets on LinkedIn or through a website like Simbi.
I'll sign up for health insurance through Affordable Care Act.	Your company's group health care is no indication (in any fraction) of how much your individual health care quote will be.	Make sure this is a real part of your analysis when thinking through the impact and trade-offs you'll make to fund your dream. Talk to a free broker early on when doing your projections.
I won't need money if I am doing what I love.	That's noble and true in many respects. However, totally abandoning financial security without a plan will eventually mess with your head if it gets too tight. If you aren't already wondering if you are in fact crazy after seeing the look of terror in your loved ones' eyes when you tell them you're cashing in your savings and your comfy job to do this fun thing, at some point you can benefit yourself by taking the blinders off. Make a true analysis of what your baby needs. Hopefully this moment comes when you challenge your financials in the business plan part of this book.	Don't be too quick to detach from the grip of what money can bring to your baby business.

to see than all the *right* reasons I had come up with. For better or worse, they were looking out for my financial future and overall peace and, while they won't admit it, were also looking out for themselves; they were fearful of having to compete for my time while I birthed this business.

I was so excited about my baby business that I forgot I was asking a lot of them and that I needed to recognize their concerns and acknowledge their many questions . . . especially from a tactical perspective. Doing so would not only help our relationship in the future, but also patch the unseen (by me) holes in my plan. Your loved ones may not know the business answers, but they do know you and they represent some relationships you will need to rely on (like when said spouse has to collect the business laundry and make the bank deposit while you're taking care of a real newborn). Even if their feedback is bogus, handling it is part of the job.

Application to Business

Relationships count. You can't do this alone. You need the buy-in from your immediate family and closest network. Don't fight them. Sell them on the business. Engage them so you can get their help. And be ready to address their concerns. They are stakeholders who will give support, which can be the foundation that leads to your success. I took my husband's willingness to "consider it" as a victory and relaxed my defenses a bit. I was able to get him to yes by stepping outside my enthusiasm in order to consider his fears. I learned that it was largely the lost income he was worried about, so I agreed to reevaluate everything after two years. That disarmed him but it also evolved me: I was practicing listening to my stakeholders while honoring my journey. This early awareness practice and stakeholder mindfulness would later buoy my business because of the experience I was selling and therefore the multifaceted talent and customers I wanted to attract.

So, after those six grueling conversations with my loving and (ahem) judicious husband, I started feeling out my close friends and family. One, because I might need some investors since my husband and I were on different planets about the importance of my concept, and two, I really needed someone to tell me they were supportive. I didn't find exactly what I was looking for here either. Instead, I found more of what I needed: lessons in how to grow a healthy layer of thick skin and perspective.

With each conversation I could more clearly articulate the offering, see the reactions of others, and deepen my belief in the business. The response was generally positive. "That's a great idea!" "That's exactly what this area needs!" "I'm excited!" "I'm inspired!" These conversations also prepared me for later, when I perfected my elevator speech. I learned to answer the negative nellies who challenged my assertions (like, guys *do* drink tea and enjoy having their feet rubbed). While I needed to hear their feedback, I also needed to appreciate that not everyone would be my customer, so this was good training. On the whole, I received the reassurance I needed to stay positive and connected to my idea. It was, however, the beginning of the end of certain friendships, some of which I'm sad about and some of which needed to happen in order to make space for more like-minded and like-hearted business kinships. More on this below.

Expect Decoupling

I had a childhood friend who always told it like it was. I adored her for that. Yet we lost touch during this period because she thought I was crazy for leaving a good job and couldn't appreciate my burning need to birth this baby. I stopped checking in with her. Creating spreadsheets and dreaming up programs to grow revenue was more rewarding than talking with someone who couldn't appreciate my exciting new world. I just didn't have space for negative energy when the thing I was creating was *so good*. Unfortunately, this happened often, which meant a fair amount of repair work when I looked up and realized that, in fact, I missed some of my friends. Connecting to my business felt good, and connecting with new people (which really came when I started networking after I came out with my news) felt incredible. New, relevant, helpful people were a godsend at that time, and I wanted to exchange energy only with them. This meant that unless the family member or friend had previously gone down this path and could speak to what I was so focused on, I found it hard to relate to them. That turned out to be a lot of people. Even my mom, who gifted me with some of my entrepreneurial wiring, had some dated advice that didn't really apply to my situation, and I found myself talking less about my baby secret when chatting with her. In time, even though I found new energy with new entrepreneurial friends, the new and shiny wore off, as it always does, and I realized that I still needed to connect to who I was and where I came from via some of the people who were still on my mind. Unlike my relationship with my spouse and to some extent my mom, these relationships could more easily look different going forward. And they did.

My friends were relationships I wanted; I *needed* those relationships with my partner and mother since their buy-in was critical to my emotional peace. It made me aware that in life (as in business) you're either growing closer or you're growing apart. Whether it's from some*thing* or some*one*. Or in my case, multiple someones. Relationships are unquestionably hard to maintain when life shifts are happening, let alone when conceiving something so consequential but has nothing to do with them. This continues to prove true at various points in life, whether it's getting married, switching career focus, or having real babies. Old friends can sometimes simply not get it or not find you fun anymore. At this tender stage in your business incubation, defending yourself in stale friendships is not good energy. Unless those relationships are the sun and moon to you, give them the space they need and recognize that any disentanglement may not only be about you.

Application to Business

Decoupling is detachment. Starting a business means turning a strategic eye to things that aren't mission critical, including toxicity in relationships. Sometimes it's writing off partners or vendors that you like personally but who aren't serving you profession-ally. Sometimes it's shutting down friendships that deplete rather than energize you. In certain circumstances, if it feels like something has to give, let it. It's not always going to be obvious (or easy) to opt out of a relationship. But business is rarely binary and is usually navigating ambiguity and awkwardness in the beginning. That said, if you need to fall back on "it's just business" to create space, do it. In friendship or bizship, you need black *and* white *and* also the gray, so think about whether a relationship is worth the navigation when the rest of the lines are blurred. This training of the brain to appreciate *both* will help, and in this practice, you get to call on your future self to help set aside reserves for the relationships that might benefit from time or distance. This space can also help guide you back to a place where you may value other points of view for the trust and depths that your relationship has attained.

It is healthy to purge anything that's not serving you, and let's face it, you're going to need all the positivity and inspiration you can get in life, baby business or not. Times of transition or difficulty are when the value of a relationship really becomes apparent. Through relation-ship evaluation, you'll learn how to ask better for what you need of people. Every person can (and should) play a different role, and you can (and will) need to call on some agreement you have. They can be a sounding board, advice giver, agree-to-give-no-advice-listener, hon-est feedback provider, or promise-not-to-talk-about-this-topic kind of relationship. This relational clarity is an important life skill, and it will come up again when honing your business senses in the evalua-tion of advice section of this book.

Some friendships sunsetted and others blossomed, like with my sister, who also started a business at the same time. Starting a busi-ness allowed this important relationship to deepen. It also unearthed a collection of people who, instead of saying I was crazy, said "let me know how I can help." I returned to this list frequently, from calling in favors on getting my "likes" up or enjoying some free design advice. The best part of this brace-yourself lesson is that the *good* friends will love you enough to be patient with your distractions and allow you the space to really enjoy this period, even finding a way to cheer you on after their initial feedback was offered.

To be*labor* the point, for me, a lot of the friends who once didn't want me to take a risk (or maybe were envious that I could), have been asking me to finish this book because even though it was hard for us as our relationships changed, they have been inspired and have opened their hearts to ideas of their own. A colleague of mine echoed this sentiment when talking about how first-movers experience a bit of resistance even among friends, because people are not programmed to embrace changes to the status quo. Most resistance to change can be traced back to fear: jealousy, frustration . . . defenses against their own emotions. The first to announce their pregnancy may not receive the enthusiastic outpouring of support because the nonpregnant friends are scared of what might happen to their tribe. Yet it's part of the life cycle. Those friends start having babies (or their own version of birthing) and although at first someone is afraid of the shift, suddenly out of nowhere they too want a baby. And so it goes, but someone has to go first and disrupt the relationship. It seems like a lot of extra work (any kind of transformation is serious work), but no rewards are fully enjoyed without dedication, and no short road stands out in the memory of a trip. The journey is long but totally worth it, as any pregnancy will reveal. When you stand back, ideally with more than just your experience or lessons, there will be immeasurable value and pride for having done something that stretched you more than you ever imagined.

First-movers experience a bit of resistance even among friends, because people are not programmed to embrace changes to the status quo.

These adjustments in the quiet early days may be unnerving, but they're rites of passage. Only in doing something hard does a powerful connection to the compass within emerge, begging you to trust her wisdom and treasure the ride of a lifetime.

Expecting: Early Moments

▶ Entrepreneurship is lonely. Prepare for a lot of thinking and self-talking to find the answers already within you.
▶ Change happens. Embrace it. It's okay if you don't recognize your new tendencies in the name of business creation.
▶ Feedback from those closest to you can be helpful, and you can learn from how you handle it.
▶ It's a long transformative road, but worth it. Your soul has been asking for this kind of rewarding experience, and it won't come without some heavy lifting

☐ Your Readiness Journal

Now having read this, marinate on where you are with your concept. In silence, sketch your business dream. Imagine your goals, determine your why. Ask yourself why you're the best person for *this* business concept and why the time is *now*. If everything is in your power, imagine what your timeline looks like.

_____

_____

_____

_____

_____

_____

_____

_____

After sketching these in delightful detail, revisit the chapter takeaways and assess where your efforts may take you in the quiet transition of bringing this concept to life.

2

Have Concept, Must Develop

$\mathcal{S}$ettling on a name for my business brought the biggest rush of dopamine. When *it* had an identity, so then did *I*. I experienced a chemical release every time I thought about not needing to do my day job much longer because I had a light at the end of my tunnel. But beyond natural rewards the body gives to keep the experience moving you along, the Universe too, favors those in pursuit of happiness. By putting so much thought and energy into something that might magnify the ordinary, and when you're in alignment with your talents and passions, I firmly believe that the forces conspire to spoon dollops of excitement to keep you going. *Doing something that makes the soul happy attracts more goodness.* The feeling of doing something purposeful, within your zone of genius cannot be replicated, and having these hits of thrill, especially while still working the day job, is incredible. It kept me going when I knew my old job, while challenging and well paid, *couldn't* be the thing that I carried on doing the rest of my life. *Especially* now my concept was growing inside me. I can point to so many rewards, even early on, like positive feedback, a growing network interested in helping, and being proud of documents or collateral I was creating to explain my business. Nothing brought a tear to my eye faster than seeing the first true signs of life: seeing it take shape in mock-ups of my logo and website or receiving my business cards in the mail. It was like seeing my baby for the first time on an ultrasound. (I can say that now that I've since had two human children.) The first time you have these signs of life are defining moments. *It's really happening!* Give the moments their place in making you feel alive with clarity.

Some things are easy to relish while some remind us that we're adapting to a big shift . . . *like morning sickness.* Adjustment phases are hard and, perfect concept or not, starting a business is one big adaptation. Adjustments are inevitable. There will be phases of development regardless of your background. Hard skills (like finance and marketing) will come in time. But today, open yourself to a new set of normal, I-should-learn-more-about-that-one-too perspective. It's difficult but important for the expecting mom. In other words, become willing to dig deeper even in areas you once felt proficient in.

Expect Evolution . . . and a Lotta Self-Improvement

Ideally, you could center on what you're good at and outsource the rest. Unfortunately, most founders aren't able to do much other than bootstrapping, so in addition to assessing strengths, it's time to get real comfortable with any areas for development. This was confusing to me because most business books, and even business school, encouraged me to hire professionals to do anything I couldn't or wouldn't do. But the truth is, I didn't have the unicorn budget for it. Thus, deeper exploration commenced to first figure out what I could (or pretend I could) do that didn't come at a huge expense to the brand or the goal. Many founders attribute success to skills like decision making (and not ruminating), being willing to start small with an eye for big, and recognizing the need to wear all the hats. Next, it's getting comfortable with the vernacular, like understanding EBITA or gross versus net income. Then it's little nuggets of wisdom you pick up along the way, like the "what would happen if" tactic used in negotiations. That one was used on me a few times and helped me realize just how steep the learning curves are. And even the areas you felt pretty strong in could feel a little inadequate now that the stakes are high. I thought the interviewing and negotiation boxes were checked as I thought about the skills this new job would require of me. I would soon find out what it meant to be a good negotiator—that my corporate HR interviewing skills weren't necessarily transferable); and my networking, following advice, and time management functioned in isolation but not nearly as well when the temperature was turned up and my vision *was* the brand. Soon I would be *the* person making *every* decision and magically get everything done efficiently. I knew I was really good at figuring things out and getting things done, but my skills needed to up-level if I was going to do *all the things* with much more efficiency and precision.

This skills assessment brought me to one of my biggest takeaways in my real life MBA (My Business Adventure), which is that my tools weren't as sharp as I needed them to be. Memorizing primers on certain subjects was a start (although not enough) but each time I had practice in a certain area, I strengthened a muscle and found greater comfort within that discipline. Put simply, my *business* needed me to excel in these topics. *Nothing personal.* While big jobs in your business, like finance and marketing, may be eventually outsourced, innate skills in everyday business cannot be easily delegated, especially in the beginning. Recognizing the importance of a skill and

---

Many founders attribute success to skills like decision making (and not ruminating), being willing to start small with an eye for big, and recognizing the need to wear all the hats.

---

where you currently stand on the proficiency scale in regard to it is a natural dichotomy to work through, and like any food aversion or morning sickness, it may take a little time to adapt. But recognizing the importance of the skill will hopefully bring a willingness to assess and adapt as you do your best to get comfortable during this adjustment phase.

Application to Business

Start with searching. You may already be good at some skills. You can still improve. You may wholly lack others, but you will learn. Remind yourself (a few hundred times) to stay cen-

*B*ecause this whole book is about increasing your comfort on this journey to birthing your concept, consider these questions to assess where you may need to develop soft skills before the more tactical skills are introduced in the next chapter.

1   Do you prefer not to make someone uncomfortable? Do you try to temper curiosity with respect for unknown boundaries?

   If you answered yes to these, plan to read the section on interviewing (page 42).

2   Are you able to focus on a conversation and what you're able to learn from the exchange? Could responding with grace be possible in disagreements?

   If you answered no to either of these, read the section on listening (page 48).

3   Can you remove emotions from situations, especially when pertaining to personal needs? Are you competitive or motivated by winning?

   If you answered no (and perhaps even if you answered yes), brush up on the negotiating skill section (page 52).

4   Do you view networking as unnecessary, superficial, or intimidating? Would you rather stay behind your computer than give your elevator speech?

   If you answered yes, review the section on networking (page 58).

tered, be patient, and know that perfection may not ever come, *certainly not in the beginning*. This applies to every single thing in business. You'll have times of clarity and times when you know the only way through is through. Honestly assessing the areas where you experience hesitation will pay dividends if you invest in strengthening early and before you actually *need* a particular skill set. Change takes time. In identifying that baseline, you'll discover what it means to push yourself and become a phenomenal swimmer in your new entrepreneurial sea. Remember that each time you practice, you become stronger, and new challenges help you grow.

---

5   When you find something you really like, do you rush to tell other people about it? Do you enjoy persuading people and derive pleasure from their satisfaction?

   If you answered no, you may not have a proclivity for sales and should consider a course in sales.

6   Are your systems flexible? Do you meet deadlines without someone to keep you accountable?

   If not, see the sections on systems) and on time management (page 71).

7   Are you good with money and budgets? Do you know exactly where your money comes from and where it goes?

   If no, plan to make money management skills an early professional development priority.

8   Do you see personalities shine through early on when working with others? Do you know what to do with work styles that are not like yours?

   If no, consider the workstyles section in this chapter.

9   How attached are you to perfectionism? Does a product have to be perfect before releasing? Are you more concerned with short-term gains than long-term successes?

   If not, see the section on resilience and stick-to-it-iveness balanced with letting go (page 88).

These soft skills will come up routinely and as the chief everything officer, only you get to flex these muscles. Building muscles only comes with practice, so get comfortable with where you are now and where you can welcome some evolution.

Undeniable Business Skill #1: Interviewing

Trusting my gut has generally served me well in life and in becoming a biz-mom. If anyone ever asks my advice, I ask first what their body is telling them, not only their head. But when it comes to interviewing (read: investing in people), the gut should only be one data point. Sure, a heavily weighted point but one that is in balance with other influences. Meeting new people can be exciting, especially when they align with your direction and can potentially get you to the next milestone quickly. Someone who fits well with your personality, energy and goals . . . look no further, right? *Not always.* What you really need might look different if you can set aside the excitement (just for a moment), because more often than not, things will get tough, and your stakeholders, employees, vendors, investors, designers, contractors, fill-in-the-blank-ers will disappoint you, or you them. This especially goes for partners. Taking some time to consider what you need in downtimes is one way to weather the storm when bringing on teammates, partnerships, and other relationships that can make your life so easy—or otherwise. Some advice that I came by the hard way is to make this process slow. You've heard the rule hire slow, fire fast. I would say that was one of the truest lessons I learned, and it came even before I started hiring employees. When hiring for yourself, it's easy to rely on personal feelings to shortcut decisions; however, going slow and asking uncomfortable questions would have saved many a difficult conversation down the road. If you choose the wrong partner, deconstructing the relationship takes more energy than simply exploring many options up front. Dig into expectations and timelines. Discuss how to work best together and through differences. Identify what you both need out of the arrangement and how you'd handle it if one party stopped pulling their weight. Be curious. Be diligent. Be intentional about your relationships as you interview, and follow these tips.

▶ **Interview multiple vendors or candidates.**

- **Do your homework to establish trust early on.** It saves so much time in the ice breaking/small talk if you know something about the person from LinkedIn, saw their website, researched their industry, and you've made a point to think about what they or their company can bring to the table. The trust you're seeking in the interview phase is multidimensional. Them of you: you're a solid person (and not spacy or ill prepared). You of them: you've confidently got a sense of what they bring to the table. And you of *yourself*: you have made the best decision that time and energy allow in that moment.

- **Ask about availability, competing demands, and their interest in working with you.** Specifically, get nosy and ask those squirmy questions: understand their family life, their client load, and what makes this a good opportunity for them. Fine print: You can't ask certain questions of potential employees about their personal situation, but you can broach the topic of outside interests and allow them to tell you about obligations pertaining to their demands. See the interview section in chapter 9 (page 223) for other great questions.

- **Talk to them about what they'd want in their contract.** It's not an *if*, it's a *when* scenario. Everyone (even your friend who is doing the work for free, or your mom who agreed to help do the books until you can afford a bookkeeper) will feel shortchanged in the arrangement. Everyone has subconscious, or even very real, ideas about how things will look for them. An email will suffice, but everyone's agreements need to be written down, and discussing what those needs are up front makes drafting the agreement more harmonious. They may need to think about it and get back to you, but make sure it's one of the first things you discuss so it's one of the first things that's done.

- **Get comfortable with the uncomfortable.** Remember, you're investing in them. I finally figured this out on my third real estate agent. The first was highly recommended by a successful colleague in the retail industry, and I liked the guy . . . except he couldn't make time to even send me properties, much less coordinate meetings to see the inside of an available space (searching for real estate in the commercial world is a different game than residential). The second only needed to let me into the space but was unable to make a single meeting we set in the span of two months. (I later discovered there was a substance-abuse situation, but not before learning how hard it was to stick up for myself in a different set of circumstances.) The third was delightful; I felt he was looking out for my best interest, but things still got contentious at the end, and I wish I'd explored all my options earlier rather than when I was out of time. I also wished I could have gotten past the "I'm new in this game" mentality and come to the interview table with confidence. Still, I was able to reflect on my recruiting and HR experiences and parlay those inquiry skills with the savvy entrepreneur skin I wanted to wear and come up with some solid questions (page 46) that were useful in multiple scenarios—bankers, employees, and assistants alike. Having asked these early on would have avoided hard conversations that kept me from my work, in a very vulnerable period of needing to make money but with a big roadblock (finding a retail space) in the way. Thankfully, I suppose, I had many more chances to try these questions on and get to the information I really needed to make effective decisions. The questions can be asked nicely and woven into conversations, or you can assert yourself and ask them however you need to; either way, remember *it's not about them or how comfortable* they *are with* you. Interviewing is about *you* and how this potential arrangement allows your growth or peace of mind. Being bold enough to ask difficult questions can encourage them to respect you more, recognizing that you'll be asking hard questions later as an incentive to keep them performing for you.

If you haven't quit your day job yet, interviewing is another example of something you could be doing while enjoying the luxury of predictable income. Remember, it's best if this process goes slow. While you might not have an ultrasound-like clear picture of your baby-to-be, interviewing for the future is a lot like envisioning the fully baked version of your barely perceptible baby business bun. These glances into your future are what you need to focus on nurturing it (and you!) the rest of the ways you'll be growing.

Questions for Invaluable Information from Professional Partners

1   How long have you worked in the industry? What distinguishes you from competition (always client facing, been a business owner themselves, etc.)?
2   How many clients do you usually work with at a given time? How many do you have now?
3   What do you look for/what makes a good deal (or partnership, etc.) for you?
4   How long does this process take? What are the milestones?
5   How do you work? Do you have colleagues or assistants who will be brought in or will you be doing the blocking and tackling? (Having a team isn't necessarily a bad thing—more people for you to contact, but knowing this versus your needs is important.)
6   How often do you work with first-time clients?
7   How would you describe your approach to work? Are you a juggler or selective with what you apply yourself to?
8   How much of your business is new versus repeat? How long does your typical deal take? (This is a trick question: the answer is however long it takes. It's about their comfort in working until the right deal is made, not about how quickly they can get the deal done. You do not want a real estate agent/professional partner who will lose patience if negotiations are drawing out longer than they'd prefer.)
9   Can you give me examples of recent business types you've signed?
10 What do your last three clients say about you and their experience working with you? (Don't forget to check references.)
11 Do you have any major trips/vacations coming up?
12 What happens if you're unavailable?

Additional questions specific to brokers/real estate agents:

1   On your approach to work (proactive, listing-driven, passive until negotiations, client-satisfaction): What is your style with aligning the

space with the business needs? How familiar are you with a client's plan/target market/financials?

2. Are you willing to speak up about comparables and piece the puzzle together, or do you prefer to have the client work independently and seek advice as needed? (First-timers really need geographic and industry expertise, so style does matter here. Note also that brokers asking to see my business plan meant this was a chance to prove how serious I was, and if they really read it and understood my target market, and maybe even offered feedback, I knew they would be vested in me alongside their goal of closing a deal.)

3. How often do you intend to provide updates? When can we expect to connect at the various stages (search/survey, site visits, letter of intent [LOI], lease negotiation)?

4. Are you willing to work multiple deals at the LOI stage? (This also tells you if they really want what's best for you or if they solely want to close deals.)

Additional questions specific to bankers:

1. What size loan do you typically offer? Is there room in your portfolio for small business loans?

2. Why do people seek you over other options (self-lending via credit cards or personal loans, for instance)?

3. What do you look for/what makes a good loan?

Many of these questions can also be asked of designers, accountants, bookkeepers, and anyone else whose involvement can impact your timeline, success, or long-term ease of work. For every person you interview, likability is only one small element. You have to appreciate them as a person as well as their characteristics as a business partner. If you truly are interviewing a business partner, I like the analogy that you need to be able to "go to bed with them." This means that you respect them, can envision what the relationship would be like once you know each other intimately, and most importantly, see the value of what you can create together.

Undeniable Business Skill #2:

Listening and Following Good Advice

Figuring out how to quiet the noise to listen to yourself or others is one thing. Deciding whose advice to follow is another thing altogether. The first part comes with time. Sharpening your listening abilities, situational awareness, and critical reasoning skills takes a little more effort. Recall the dated advice my mom gave; it was hard for me to appreciate her perspective on best ways to finance when she did her books in an actual ledger (technology came online toward the end of her business run). Her suggestions to research a home equity line of credit instead of a traditional business loan was spot on but so hard to hear because I felt her advice may be antiquated. Besides, no one really knows as much about your business as you do, and if any advice is contrary to what you're already thinking, or it's unsolicited, it will simply be hard to hear. *How could formulated perspective come from anyone who hasn't thought through this concept a thousand ways to Thursday?* I call this "entrepreneurial stonewalling," where being so tied to your project you feel that receiving hard love is harder than many are willing to accept, even in the name of love, and shutting yourself off to any other suggestion is a natural defense. New relationship dynamics, exposing yourself to new people with different backgrounds or experiences, and the directly relevant advice out there makes the tendency to ignore advice enticing. Fortunately, listening to your grounded self is also an option that works. But in reality, if this is your first business, someone's outside perspective could transform your thinking or approach. How do you know when it's time to tune in? Be in the habit of evaluating advice and the process of listening will feel easier. Consider the following:

▶ Do you need advice or just to talk out loud? Taking a moment to seek the answers within you often results in coming up with your own opinion that might feel more fitting.

- Are you in a place to receive the advice/is it related to a challenge you're ready to face?
- Is the source relevant to your business? Are they conflicted? Is their advice emotion or fear based? Does the person have something to gain from giving you this advice?
- Does it make sense?
- Have you heard it before? If you've heard it from a few people, then it is worth considering.
- Do you need a second (or third or fourth) opinion? If it's important enough to seek advice, it is important enough to seek more than one view.
- What will the outcome look like in three minutes/three months/three years? It may help you figure out which aligns more with your goals or may be a fleeting idea that won't really add value or momentum.
- Will the results heed the 80/20 rule? Will 80 percent outcome come from 20 percent of energy invested in the idea or advice? If not, it's probably not a good idea.
- Can you see the *yes!* in the decision? If not, it's probably a no.

I had received advice to make my own infused sugars to go along with the teas I sold, as an additional revenue stream. It worked during the early days when we were gaining momentum, but storage, production, packaging, and supply made it difficult to maintain once the higher margin areas of my business took off. Scrapping the idea felt right because I was thinking about the three-year-old business rather than the three-month-old business. It did not create enough revenue to make it worth the distraction.

An advice sorter I often go to is picturing myself sitting on the board of my business. Boards usually represent a diverse set of views and backgrounds and can bring a holistic approach to business decisions. You should have one even if it's an informal feedback group. A collection of different personalities and perspectives (still relevant to business) who you can call on regularly (and they call on you for feedback as well) will carry you through some lonesome days. I had about six different friends to whom I would regularly take ideas. They were like my advisory board, though I never got them in the same room together. They brought different experiences and thoughts unlike my own on most topics, and I could count on them for a perspective I usually hadn't thought about or a lens I hadn't yet applied. If you take this approach, you'll start to see whose sound advice fits best with you and you'll go more selectively to the same people over time.

Welcoming advice is part of the journey. The sooner you develop shortcuts to deciding how to seek advice, the sooner you get feedback and the sooner you get to decide if you've heard enough consistent feedback to take action. Inaction is expensive. A lot of people have the

Biz Tip
You are going to be flooded with advice and feedback from the outside. Don't let this deluge of fact and fiction hold you back from what you're setting out to do.

urge to problem-solve, and you may have to reject advice that simply doesn't fit with your model or your worldview. That's okay. It's simply data and worth considering for even a brief moment. Learn who you can trust and draw boundaries on the advice department for everyone else. If you don't want advice from everyone, best not to talk details to everyone. Consider offering only positive updates on your project to keep their advice at bay and your good energy echoing.

But seek advice for important decisions, even if you don't follow it. Your trusted circle may have answers, but keep in the back of your mind that the unbiased perspective of a coach may be worth the consultant fees, especially when you get beyond the bootstrapping phases. Even knowing it's an option can allow enough space to make a decision without too much extra noise.

Undeniable Business Skill #3: Negotiating

Some tenants pay less rent than others. Some people pay less for their car than you paid for yours. Why? Because they were better at negotiating. Even small advantages can make or break your business. So, how can you capture these advantages for your baking business bun? Practice separation. I had studied negotiations in business school and bargained for best solution in my previous career in human resources. But until it was personal, like *my* savings and reputation hitched to outcomes, it wasn't really negotiating. There's a very intimate relationship between you and your business and it's difficult to separate the two, but during negotiations (and generally), you have to be willing to practice distancing yourself from your business. Your business, the labor of love that you pour so much solitary effort into, is very personal. So when you have to ask for something or demand the best for your baby, it's really hard not to intensely feel blows or rejection. Practicing separating yourself will pay dividends. It will never be a perfect separation because of the cord that connects you to your creation, but here are some separation techniques you can draw upon.

- ▶ Visualize you as separate from your business. Draw a picture if you have to—it sounds hokey, but there's science around visualizations and firing neuron pathways to change your mindset.
- ▶ Write down what life is like for you outside of your business. Recognize you are indeed a person and not entirely dependent on this business. A fun way to do this is to do the seven lenses game (seven lenses through which you see the world: mom, problem solver, sister, daughter, etc.). It's a quick way to reconnect with you as a person separate from your business.
- ▶ Think about what other business owners do when they need to move the needle. Channel a mentor or someone who is a "boss" in your mind and try on some of their language, -isms, and approaches for a day. If you're in touch with them (not just

an inspirational mentor), maybe give them a call and hear how they'd approach an upcoming negotiation.

Once you've made peace with the distinction of you from your business, brace yourself for the tactical elements of negotiations. Negotiations usually don't feel awesome, but as best as you can, strive for a yes! feeling. Anything less and you're starting your project with the same feeling as going to work with spit-up on your shirt. Recognize that *yes!* may not be everything you asked for, but it could mean feeling enthusiastic and satisfied about a deal where you get most of what you need. My sister opened her yoga studio shortly after I opened my tea shop. She is a beast when it comes to negotiations. She was a career salesperson who did not understand the word no; it didn't exist in her vernacular. She negotiated against the biggest fish in our area's landlord sea, and even with a lawyer on her side, still wound up with a deal that was largely in the landlord's favor. She learned a lot, specifically how to keep a long-range view in critical moments and that everyone has to protect their own interests. What she had to decide was whether she would rather be *finally* pursuing her dream, albeit with a constricting lease that some days would feel like a nightmare, or be sad to walk away from her dream but have freedom to conjure something new, without a personal guarantee and a ten-year lease. She does have a good thing going now, five years into the business and on renegotiated terms, but her early experience reminds me that even the best of us need to negotiate harder. Her strengths couldn't have fully compensated for her lack of knowledge about commercial leases, complicated by the pull to do whatever she needed to do for her concept to come to life. This is where a lot of first-time entrepreneurs falter.

Negotiations usually don't feel awesome, but as best as you can, strive for a yes! feeling.

They often think they're taking a hit on negotiations for the good of bringing their baby to life, yet it's critical to not easily concede a negotiation point without considering the short- and long-term impact on the business. It is contrary to your natural instinct to keep moving forward, but here too, is an opportunity to evolve your thinking. Even the most experienced mama sometimes has adjustment periods (that lovely morning sickness), so remember that discomfort means there is growth.

The good news is that you learn quickly that it's not about you or your vulnerabilities: business *is* business when it comes to negotiations. I will argue it's not so simple in other areas of biz parenthood, but in negotiations, the personal elements can be removed if you try. The sooner you can get over yourself and any fear of rejection, the more energy you'll save. Remember:

- ▶ You never know until you ask.
- ▶ Focus on the outcome, not your feelings. It's for your business, your employees (current or future), funding your kids' vacations, or whatever your goals are. It's about an outcome, not about you.
- ▶ Ev-er-y-thing is negotiable. From Fedex to fixed fees for services. Recognize that the other party is going for their best-case scenario, and you should ask for yours. No one goes into negotiations giving you a bone or some other freebie that matters to them. The worst that can happen is they say no. You may have to find another option that works better for you, but in today's innovation economy, there will always be another option if a negotiated middle ground isn't attainable.
- ▶ Prepare! Second chances are rare. Retrading is awkward. Think: *Your future depends on how honest you are with your needs in this moment.* Before starting, know what you need and have an equally acceptable backup solution (BATNA planning: Best Alternative to a Negotiated Agreement). Other

preparations include thinking about ways you can bundle services, or sometimes even barter, that may be of interest to the other party.

▶ Don't tip your hand too early. Information is power and if you show all your cards or reveal too much about your stakes (e.g., by taking the first pass at the LOI or showing your financials before they're invested in the idea of working with you), they may walk away quickly. Clearly state early on what your limits are (budget, timeline, etc.), but don't tell them everything about your situation or vulnerabilities.

▶ Based on initial minimum requirements (goals, budget limits), you'll soon know if it's a workable option. Try not to waste anyone's time if it's not a fit.

▶ When in verbal talks, remember to breathe. Count to three before you respond.

▶ Look ahead three months or three years before you sign/agree. Play the 'would you rather' game that my sister did: Would you rather have this behind you and deal with the risks, or take a little longer to assuage any fears?

▶ Be prepared to walk away. While getting to a deal feels good, walking away does too, especially if the stakes are high.

I had been searching for a location for over ten months, finally found the property, then spent several weeks agreeing to the terms of the LOI. When that was finally signed, the lease negotiations began, and I researched local zoning requirements on operating in that space (drinking fountains, types of allowable egress, and many facets of code pertaining to the Americans with Disabilities Act [ADA]). I learned that I would need to install a ramp and an elevator lift, and both ADA-accessible restrooms needed to be on the first floor. That reduced my 1,500-square-foot footprint to around 900 square feet of usable space, and the first floor had only about 200 square feet before you needed to hike up the ramp to get to the more open space. I couldn't realize my dream in such a squished configuration, and I had to walk away. It was hard. I had spent weeks going back and forth on every element of the LOI, committed to making it work. I was so invested after all that time, evaluating my needs, researching, and promising followers that "we're close!" to finally opening the store—not to mention my dwindling savings—that I literally needed to spend a week regrouping. But it was the right move. The extra money spent on just getting the doors open would have choked cash flow and thus, the business.

The good news is that the landlord was invested in me too (because I had been calling and asking to be let in fifteen different times to try and measure various ways of Tetris-ing big bathrooms sideways) and requested that I consider another space in the same building, all on one floor but smaller than I had initially planned. Reconfigured from my fantasy but yes, I could make it work after hiring an architect to help measure the code requirements and layout possibilities. We got to a balanced deal and finally, sweet moment of glory, had an address.

Successful negotiations can also take the form of smaller victories. Opening a retail store meant numerous credit card processors and vendors knocking (literally) on my door. Even with vendors seeking out customers, everyone wants a personal guarantee, and only when a business is well established and has a reputable credit score does the entity *sometimes* help secure the financial relationship. Most often, it's you, personally backing any business obligation. These show up in many ways, like signing on with a gateway exchange company between the cloud terminal and the credit card companies (everyone wants to make sure they're getting paid, with few contested fees), or payroll companies wanting to make sure you're on the hook if your business account doesn't cover payroll, or even suppliers asking you to be on the hook if your business check bounces. I mention these to remind you that because *you* are in charge, it's *your* name on the line, and you can pull levers to make these relationships work better for you. In fact, a good number of vendors were okay with me simply crossing out the personal guarantee language in their contracts.

It's not so different when negotiating with clients, either. There is still the same separation from the personal you need to make; the same awareness of your worth or expertise, long-term trade-offs, and your willingness to walk away. Additionally, embracing the attitude that a loss today may still be a win tomorrow can help when seeking mutual respect and good karma. You are investing in a future relationship, when more resources are hopefully available.

Business Skill

Once you start talking about your baby business, it's naturally the only thing you want to talk about, since what you focus on only grows in your mind. Having a concept or a product that you know people will love is exhilarating. Having strangers also get excited for it and then meeting new people who think creatively all day long is intoxicating and enlivening. Goodness starts to flow, like attracts like, and when you're experiencing invigoration, fulfillment, and exhilaration energetically, you can attract people and opportunities to help you along and light up your path. *This* is the ultimate goal of networking. Too bad there's this tiny other commitment you have, called starting a business; otherwise it would be amazing to feel the networking vibes all day long!

To the volume-driven entrepreneur, a basic goal of networking can be to meet as many people as you possibly can, early on. I've heard this called "grin and grab" networking. While it's fun to meet dreamers and doers and it may be a strategy you employ, keep in mind that there's a trade-off in networking. To have a good client, referral, or mentor, you have to work at it, and the work starts *after* the networking event. All of those cards collected under the basic goal of casting a wide net means a whole lot of work now that you're home. Speed networking like this means you may not have had a chance to connect with anyone on a deep level, but if you did, those are the folks in whom to invest your follow-up efforts. Follow-up can look like thanking them for the time/energy they shared with you at the event and offering a way you can support each other; suggesting meeting for coffee to get to know them better; and keeping them warm, depending on how relevant they are to you (and you need to be to them). For instance, even if you meet only three people at an event you want to take further action on, that's three more thoughtful thank-yous at twenty minutes each (ten minutes on their site or LinkedIn, ten minutes writing a follow-up), then potentially another hour each meeting with them, with unknown returns on your time investment.

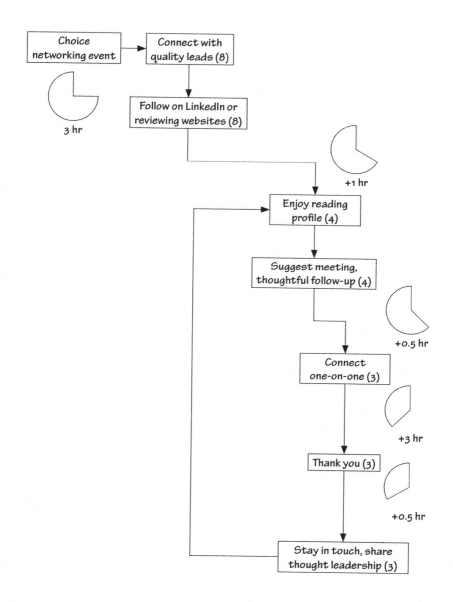

Networking Flowchart
Allot time from ongoing marketing bucket to stay relevant to your network.

Excluding the one networking event, you've spent roughly four hours on three people. Hopefully the relationship will eventually become something that energizes you, but that's a fair amount of work and illustrates the need for being intentional. Let your business needs and your "bandwidth" for follow-up be your guide. Deeper connections are better than casting a wide net, and having a few people who know you well enough to refer business to you is so much better than 100 people who can only recognize your face. Recommendations *are* the name of the business game. Those facial recognition guys will rarely be your client or mentor, so my best advice is to do the deep connecting, but with a strategy to make it worth your precious time. In building your networking strategy, consider these five W's to networking:

Who: There are a lot of people and a lot of reasons for them to be out networking, and not everyone will be helpful to you. Think about what you need when trying to figure out who you want to meet. Early on, I wanted to meet as many people as I could, so found results in meeting natural connectors who could invite me to their events and then tell me what the scene was in town (e.g., all the female biz supporters tended to appear at certain circles, versus the investors and bankers who tended to show up at other events). Because I wanted a mix in my strategy, I needed to know who went where. You learn pretty quickly which events have the folks who want the same from their networking experience as you, and you can align with them as your time becomes limited. There are a lot of overly enthusiastic entrepreneurs out there who are more about promoting their brand than building a company. And while those folks serve a purpose and may be very kind and likable, try to center on your needs: it could be a specific type of client or perhaps a like-minded soul to lift you up or hold you accountable to your goals.

It's okay if you're not attracted to certain groups, and you very well could collect a sample board of directors who bring some unique perspective just by spending time at a co-working office or through a volunteer position. Plenty of my colleagues have enough friends that refer them business that they choose not to network, and that's worked for them. I do think you should spend at least some energy networking, if only to push yourself a little (to become better at your pitch or to think bigger about complementary businesses to potentially partner with). Yet every time you hear "Oh I have a friend you should talk to," that's the sound of a possibility for a deeper connection, because your own network can help filter the best folks to work with you. Not every recommendation will be good, but a good one will last a lot longer when it came from a friend or someone you interact with regularly.

What: Did you know that someone needs to see or hear about you seven times before they take action? That's a lot of times to get in front of the same person, unless you explore multiple vehicles, where eventually you do start to gain traction. There's social, educational, accountability, business referral, and speed/power networking, to name a few types of traditional vehicles. Most traditional networking will at least offer a place to exchange cards, see a contact list of members, or form a circle and say what you do to help facilitate the exchanges. Some networking is industry-specific, which helps you stay relevant, get to know your competition, learn from each other, or be inspired. The downside is that you'll spend precious free time inside a box of like-minded individuals competing for the same customer. As with most things, there are trade-offs. The *what* of networking equals *what are you hoping to achieve:* Accountability? Inspiration? Fifty new followers? Five new sales pipelines? For me, before signing up for an event I always connected it to a current or near-term goal. I defined what I needed out of anything that pulled me away from working on my business in a concrete way, because let's face it, bootstrapping isn't congruent with paying event entry fees or allocating tons of time (which equals money), so I also regarded any time I left the house as networking. Leaving the solitary walls of my office meant I brought not just my business cards but also the intent to strike up a conversation with a stranger. In general, I consider most interactions as networking, although not in a sleazy, make-every-moment-profitable way. Rather, taking the view that you never know who is out there, and if the opportunity is natural and there is interest in what you are working on, you should be prepared. It's a bit like dating: You have to at least put yourself out there or the Universe can't meet you. It's still always to the positive because if this guy doesn't work out, he may have a more compatible brother. And if you handle it with care, he may still refer his friends to you when they need a rock star _____ (fill in the blank future you).

You never know where a conversation may lead you. Your neighbor, who already cares for you on some level because they see you every day, can be a potential source when they know what you're up to. When it comes to networking, remember it's quality over quantity, and quantity by no means equals quality.

Ice Breaker Questions Even for Introverts

All you need is a few rotating questions that can really crack into someone's zone of conversation. Here are a few that I liked in the beginning, but I encourage you to try on a few and swap them out if they start to feel stale.

1 How long have you been on your business journey? (rather than "What's your business?")
2 If you weren't (read name tag for business), what would you be doing?
3 What aspect of the agenda brought you out tonight?
4 Which CRM (customer relationship management) or project management tool do you use?
5 What trends or blogs or podcasts are you currently following?

When: You can start networking early on once you have your business cards. Your confidence ratchets up a notch or two when you're able to stand on the other side of that gorgeous business card and say, "I'm your answer." After hearing yourself say it, you will believe it, come what may. Also, I'd recommend having at least a splash page on your website by the time you set out to network, so people can look your company up when they get home. It helps jog their memory of who you were or what you talked about if you have a webpage that at least introduces the problem your company is solving, and the extra imagery will help solidify their memory of you.

Get your website/splash page up before heading out to network.

Timeline Tip

Keep in mind that there are seasons to networking that don't always mirror the seasons of your business. Consistently showing up at the same events will help people recognize you, but if you need to ease off the gas and focus your energy elsewhere, this is entirely natural. If, however, you find networking helps your revenue or your social nature, don't stop! Besides being harder to justify starting up again later, you can lose a lot of momentum by stopping altogether. It's like exercise: Even if you can only get in a ten-minute jog, it's better for your bod than doing nothing. Depending on sales pipelines, deadlines, or overwhelming tasks, the pull to take a break may exist, but listen to yourself and balance the pull with the average weight of the time it takes to secure a customer. You may very well need to nurture the sales funnel and contacts to avoid cliffs in your revenue.

When you start seeing the same people over and over again without serious leads or some spiritual motivation, it might be time to shift networking gears. When this happened, I would throttle my usual efforts and ask a friend to invite me to their BNI (Business Networking International) or other fresh venue. I would give it a few months, and when I went back to my old events, there were usually fresh faces or inspiring friends I had missed. So don't give up entirely unless you have another option that suits your needs better. Trusting that you know what you need when you set out to network will help it be fun and effective. Once you are in the right networking pools, I believe that solutions to your challenges or questions are never more than two contacts away. This is what flow of networking is, and it does feel good.

On average, do no more than one group networking event (including smaller meetings) a week when you're starting out, especially if you're still in early concept phases. One a week is arguably aggressive if you have kids or other obligations. Because of all the work that comes post event, your networking allocation expands pretty quickly. Virtual networking will save commute time but can't replace hours of face-to-faceengagement.

Why: You don't have to network like a boss, but you do need to network. Reach out to the people you know and ask who they know, especially when you're looking for something specific. Be verbal about what you're doing, but with awareness, particularly on social media. Too much business on social media is a quick way to lose your audience, so be cognizant of showmanship and "come buy from my business" versus asking for help and sharing because you're both human and you care about them as customers. The *why* of networking is of the same fiber as *how to* network in that so much comes down to message. You are networking to get your message out. You are meeting people because you need or want them under your umbrella. Your elevator pitch will need to change to appeal to your audience since they're your biggest advertisers now. Your elevator pitch (and arguably a bit of your identity) is about to have a seismic shift: It's not about *what you do* anymore. Now it's about *why* you're doing it and *how* you're going to make a difference among existing industry options. To validate this, check out Simon Sinek's TED Talk *How Great Leaders Inspire*, where he urges that "people don't buy what you do, they buy why you do it," and the best way to help them like you and your product is to get out and tell your *why* story and tell it well. Plainly put, you're going to need to justify what you're doing from here on out, and that's a natural pairing with selling yourself (not to mention the responses you'll get: doubt, excitement, interest, sneering . . .). Now that you're repping yourself without the comfort of an established corporate company name behind you, it feels and arguably is like you have to validate your very existence. Engage with your message via the pitch, and really believe the pitch, even if your mentality is that you're still faking it till you make it. The best story you tell about yourself is the story you tell to yourself. Believe that you're *the* solution to some real problems. Also, remember that you can't sell to everyone and by embodying this acceptance in your pitch, you can become more of a loving option for them and not a forced relationship. People don't want to be sold to; they want to connect, so bringing it back to loving energy via your message will carry you farther during quick networking exchanges.

Pro Tip

Even if your business cards are inexpensive, don't hand them out to just anyone. You can very easily have a conversation without indicating that you wish to continue the conversation by giving them a card. Protect your time and simply thank them for the chat. It's totally okay to say, "Let's look to talk more at the next event" if you're not feeling sparks right then and there. Save your cards and your follow-up energy for the chase you want for your business dream. And don't stress if you weren't in their networking cards—their goals are out of your control and pleasing everyone is impossible and impractical.

Where: Location can and should be dictated by what you can afford. Venues like Chamber of Commerce come not just with monthly dues but usually event fees. BNIs, while selective and expensive, can make a difference for many folks because they rely on chapter members to refer business to you. That means you have more than twenty people trying to help you, but you also do this for them in return, every week. Speaker-led events, while usually powerful and pricey, might help weed out less serious networkers or those less focused on building a brand than getting some fast leads. It is worth considering if the subject matter or audience is relevant to you. Some networking costs are good investments. I only went to free or high-ROI events in the early days, but when cash flow was positive and I chose to step away from the business to network, I preferred speaker-led events because I needed to be inspired and be social with like-spirited energies. For $40 a month I could be motivated, connect to bigger ideas, and gain built-in accountability groups. Money well spent. Being in a room with a handful of highly effective, helpful, inspiring, high-potential individuals where you have good conversations is a win, but it is exhausting. Exhausted is not depleted, though, so notice the difference, and if it's the latter then it's time to change venues. No matter whether it's a dinner party or a large crowd, it's worth your time if you feel uplifted or energized about your venture when you get home. If, instead, you feel depleted, which is easy when networking, you may want to shift your crowd.

Even if your networking strategy is mostly virtual, focus on the relationship at some point, because people tend to better trust someone they've met in person or have worked with and made an impression on. Some network organizations have private Facebook groups, so you can still be as relevant as possible without attending in person. I encourage you to block no more than one of your weekly networking hours to virtual networking. (This is different from your posting, as you'll see in the marketing section, page 105.)

One last point on the *where* of networking: Some professions view mass distribution (mailers or email blasts) as networking. While it is a marketing strategy, farming blasts are not to be confused with actual relationship building. Get out from behind the collateral and share your enthusiasm with another person, and see where that exchange can carry you.

Goal	Venue	Purpose	Impact
Meet specific professional (copy editor, broker, etc.)	BNI, Chamber of Commerce, or female entrepreneur meetup	Focused event connecting entrepreneurs with each other or service providers	Usually at a cost of $20–$50 per event
Find as many potential customers for my pipeline as possible	Mass networking event like Women in Business conference or trade show	Shower the world with your business cards…and sleep for days after	A broad reach but lots of follow-up work given volume and likelihood that connections were at the surface (will need to work to find synergy once you're home)
Meet a mentor or potential board member to improve my mission	Networking group that may have a speaker or education series or accountability measure like Her Corner, Vistage, or Cadre	Meet the people who are serious about business mastery or self-mastery, and chances are they may have some wisdom to share	Usually highest end of networking range ($40–$150 per event), but quality of inspiration is palatable
Meet a natural connector to introduce me to suppliers in my industry or tell me where I should be networking, given my ideal client	EventBright events where colleagues are planning to go, or find the person with the biggest circle around her at an event and she's probably a connector	Find the networking guru in your area who can tell you where to go for your needs; they love their connector talent; so don't feel bad asking for direction	Find ways to bring good things back to this person— sweets, lunch, referral business are all ways to say "You really made a difference for my journey"

This document is not something to manage to, but do keep it in mind as new events pop up, along with what you're willing to trade off when you look at the big picture.

Networking is a beautiful way to authentically grow your reach, your support team, and your business. You'll never know if you're meeting a good client or a good mentor, but you'll start to recognize your "people" as you regularly invest in this activity. I'd get so tickled when I walked into a room of successful business people who'd say, "Oh, you're the tea lady, I've heard of you!" That started to happen a few months in, and it had everything to do with my deeper connections talking about me as they did their own networking. Give your connections a good story about you to share. I was young and creating a different and risky concept. I was willing to talk about the startup experience stories in case someone else had been down that path. While they may not have had answers, they'd mention me to their friends: "Oh, there's someone here opening a retail space serving tea. She may have some insights and may be good to partner with." In addition to offering stories or fun updates in my networking to help stay front of mind, I would also ask what I could do for them. Then, at times, I would get the question in return and respond with whatever I needed in that moment. Even though they had their own networking to do, I was somewhere in the back of their minds. And beyond being a good citizen, these helpful exchanges deepen loyalty in both directions.

Plenty of people are relentless at networking because look at what it can do for you! But you can be tenacious and still tactful. You can doggedly chase a relationship, but they don't have to feel your aggression. One way to do this is to not assume that someone who gives you their card wants to stay in close connection with you via your mailing list. One thing I would do is separate the cards I got into two piles. One for people to keep warm (one-on-one meetings or thoughtful/helpful emails that follow on from your conversation) and one for the people who recently gave me their card but their face was blurry at best (for whom I'd at minimum connect with them on LinkedIn). On occasion, I would run into them again and then go dig their card out of pile #2 and assume the Universe has something in store if I just do the work and move them into the #1 pile. Neither pile was added to my mailing list without their permission. If it was a good connection, they'd usually sign themselves up anyway by using my email sign up link in my signature block in our correspondence. Another way to authentically but assertively manage the relationship is to be timely with your follow-up. Convention says it's less than twenty-four hours, but I say it's within the window of 'I valued our connection enough to put down my work and thank you,' which is something like twenty-four to seventy-two hours to stay relevant and remembered.

Perhaps not in your networking strategy but a good overall tip is to make sure that you're not the one bringing the negative stories. There is a time to ask for perspectives in your problem solving, and there is a time to set your business aside and listen or help solve problems for a fellow business mama. Bottom line, nurture your energy exchanges: If someone inspires you, bring that light back to them or to someone else. It's good for your practice of inviting good energy to you, and it's good for the depths your networking efforts can reach. Above all, enjoy the synchronicity of meeting like-minded people and the compounding energy to attract even more of that goodness to you. *And the beautiful signs of life continue.*

Genuinely point to a specific topic to discuss further. You may be one of a hundred of the same profession in their CRM, but having struck a personal chord in you will help them want to carry on the conversation to see where it may lead. Try not to be too pushy in your follow-up, but instead, consider inviting them to an upcoming event, or share with them some thought leadership that brought them to mind when you heard/read the information. If you do want to meet imminently (versus merely staying in touch until some relevant purpose to meet surfaces), offer two dates and then set it down. If they don't respond, put them on your list of quarterly touch bases, but ensure the outreach doesn't have much to do with selling your product or service. You're establishing that you're a trusted source, you value them as a person, and don't just view them as pipeline potential. And remember it's okay to not be in their cards or timing if they never return correspondence; the next opportunity is better suited anyway.

Undeniable Business Skill #5:
Time Management and Organization

Business Skill

There's a reason I help people create systems to make their business life easier, and it's because despite being naturally organized (since keeping a busy job, night school, and starting a business wasn't getting done on a mess of sticky notes), I still learned the hard way that more is better in this department. I still learned about really slowing down and thinking harder about my own methodology. Why did it matter? Because I was now managing much more than one person's output. The business was its own engine with many workstreams and cogs, and I had to delegate my lower priority lists—to whom, I did not yet know—but I needed to separate the tasks to keep a strategic mind in place and function at my highest. I had to determine the best tools for time management, organization, and, as much as I stammer over this word, structure of my days. There is a difference between organized and structured, and the latter seemed incongruous with my hippie proclivities and free spirit. But that same spirit also needed me to achieve some pretty big things, so I learned that getting myself A+ organized would ease my business parenthood. Proper setup is something so simple, but it can deliver so much flow of riding a rainbow of good times. Lord knows, that rainbow will vanish. There will be plenty of holes and fires, but feeling good about where your files are, how your meeting notes integrate into your CRM, how your task list works in tandem with your invoicing, or your overall process and the ways the bones of your business connect, the more with it you'll feel and the more you'll invite that vibe back to you.

Get yourself organized early, and don't spend too much time in any one area of your business only to create bigger neglect hurdles due to lack of thoughtful prioritization.

Entrepreneurs come in many forms, from the mad scientist to the highly organized. Even the most organized entrepreneur still struggles with incomplete or inefficient systems because many startups cannot afford to build systems that bridge their gaps perfectly. But try you must. The reason it's so important is because you'll soon be wearing every hat imaginable: the bill payer (passwords, logins, and receipts to track in order to categorize appropriately) and accounts receivable, the newsletter copy editor (and the different ways the content needs to speak to your blog and your social media, and the keywords that go into the site and search engine optimization [SEO] . . . and still stay interesting); the product packager and shipping department; the event planner; the researcher to find similar content to your followers; the experimenter of new products/R&D; the partnership or procurement department (finding new vendors and testing them out), the legal team (ok, try to hire this out unless you're a trained law practitioner) . . . and it goes on. No system or robot does it perfectly, so depending on who you are and how you organize your thoughts, there are various systems available. And once you have your life *mostly* in optimized fashion, you'll want to leave a little space for . . . life. A colleague of mine has outsourced most things around her business (such as a personal laundry service and automated bill paying), such that when she is required to do something that isn't driving her business, there's an immediate sense of frustration. An *awareness* of over programming your days is helpful here. Life will happen. Every day, in fact. Planning for all the CEO functions will fill up your schedule. But leaving some space for what else may come will help increase satisfaction and keep overwhelm at bay. Finding beauty in non-ideal tasks is another way to build some relaxation into your week. It's a lovely thing to be mostly in control, and it's even more beautiful to be able to let go of control, so in addition to programming your busy life to allow for them, I'd recommend thinking of some "be with what is" mantras. If you find yourself repeating them more than is healthy for an infant business to flourish, you may want to consider reevaluating what you're saying yes to or layering on top of your existing priorities.

If you're in a practice of being with what is (accepting your thoughts/fears), stress related to time to get it all done will be less frequent or less intense or both.

Mantras for Moving Forward and Acceptance

▶ What is truly necessary? Where is my purpose in this?

▶ If there is no problem, then what is here?

▶ Just look at all this abundance!

▶ It's not a problem, it's a portal (look for the opportunity).

▶ Creation can take time (while looking at a picture of the Earth)

▶ How can these tasks evolve me? Choose the ones with the biggest return first.

▶ Obstacles that are getting in the way *are* the way.

▶ Are my thoughts around this useful?

As for tactical advice on time management, there are three key things:

1 Grace: You're simply going to do your best until experience teaches you efficiency, your true demands, and how important it is to create space to manage the extras (the hard lessons in overdoing it).

2 Embrace shapes: blocks and pies.

3 Time tracking: especially for things that are easy to get lost in, and to balance the priorities of starting a business.

In other words, marketing is important, but is it more important than generating invoices? The amount of energy dedicated to it should follow the level of importance it holds for your business, and it is hard to really get a handle on the ratios without setting out for a percentage of time and then monitoring it. Is reading emails all that important? Only if it relates to the categories of your business that warrant the most amount of time based on the goals you've set. Save it for when you've finished tending to the things that really drive your revenue or sanity.

Structuring Your Day/Week

Fact or fiction? You wanted autonomy and no restrictions or micro-management in your old life, such that entrepreneurship seemed like one sweet life box checked? *Almost always fact.* I have entrepreneurial friends who nearly break out in hives when I suggest blocking calendars and committing to it like it's a business meeting. But part of being an entrepreneur is to report to no one, including your calendar . . . until you have investors, of course. I'm telling them and you, we are cyclical creatures and you can ground in rhythm. Structure doesn't have to be synonymous with constriction, and in fact, it can actually give you freedom. Blocking tasks for their importance to the business will keep you moving and sane. When you feel out of control, at least you can reconnect with your *why* and put one foot in front of the other by having some success blocks along the week. By blocking time, you set your own boundaries around time or access from others, and you owe it to your business and your sanity to establish healthy parameters on your work, since even the fun stuff is work. *Thinking* is work, yet if you're contemplating how you'll get that blogpost to pop while you know that in two hours you'll be dealing with it, the thought can be tabled or put in the notes of that block on your calendar and addressed in two hours. Productivity consultant David Allen wrote in his book *Getting Things Done*, "Your mind is for having thoughts, not holding them," and your business needs all the creative brain capacity possible. I followed the rhythm of my calendar and found freedom to do other things that I needed or wanted to. To elaborate, I always made time for marketing on Mondays, website on Wednesdays, and finance on Fridays. I left Tuesday and Thursday open to freestyle for admin and strategy, but at least three days a week I was doing dedicated work for those important things during my working hours. (There's a graphic on page 76.) Each month I had certain goals (resolve an IT issue, update contracts and intake forms, research solutions to laundry or supply chain pain points, etc.) and those would get blocked into my calendar. Every day I moved around goals or priorities and created three calendar entries to accomplish that day. Admittedly, some days even three was a stretch. Under this model, whatever marketing effort I decided on (if it was a Monday) would be one of those things. If something was missed due to unforeseen circumstances, I could always pop it over to another open window in the week. Yet if it was a priority, it was on the calendar and not on a list of tasks or ideas. I used my open/freestyle days for a little bit of strategy (and always a little bit of space-clearing admin to-dos). If I had down time, I would look at the running list in Asana, which had things like "thoughtful response to customer complaint," "review resumes for hopeful hires," "catch up with Grandma." My time was in alignment with my goals, and my priorities reflected my purpose. Suddenly I felt in control of the mess that is management of entrepreneurship. And if I finished early, I got to check my email or other to-do list. I realistically approached my day, three goals at a time, and felt like I was serving my business, because each week I made time to be deliberate. Each month, I also blocked time for goal evaluation, employee engagement, or doing something for the community. In my world of entrepreneurship and management of all the things, if I didn't protect the time, it got added to the list and didn't get done. So structuring felt good since the goal was so important. Also rewarding was the mental space that creating actual space afforded. Space to make decisions. Space to feel good about those decisions. Decision fatigue (near cousin to analysis paralysis, discussed later) is a real thing and a fast train to burnout. You know it's happening when you want someone else to decide, and it comes on quick. You're loving being boss, you're feeling what you came here for, and suddenly, you don't know . . . and how *could* you know? . . . and who else could know? And the insecurity cycle of doubt returns. Talk about inefficiency. Structuring *is* in fact security. Freedom, confidence, faith in your decisions . . . and elevating your frequency.

	Sunday	Monday	Tuesday	Wednesday	Thursday	Friday	Saturday
AM	church or brunch or some-thing sacred	marketing	(free: strategy)	website	(free: strategy)	walking meeting (rotate guest)	(sleep in); drop in at store for morale for 2–3 hours
Lunch		yoga	one-on-one lunch	goal progress (month and week)	yoga	working lunch— emails	life (laundry, groceries, etc.)
PM		opera-tions	produc-tions/ fulfillment		produc-tions/ fulfillment	finance	
After hours	weekly goal setting		cardio	networking	cardio		

Lists are important, but it's what you do with them that drives change. Without a lens of "doing" on your calendar, business moms can risk drowning in the list. Turning my project management list "top three" into calendar blocks meant that when I got an unplanned call from a vendor, I could say I'm free for the next seven minutes and safeguard the upcoming block. Sure, some days (okay, many days) are not in your control and that block of time can get shifted to later and later in the day. But scheduling meetings on top of what would be protected time means that valuable aspect of your business is likely to never get the attention it deserves. Get it on the calendar, then only true emergencies can sneak in. While not always ideal in the consulting world, blocking for at least some tasks can cut down on the number of meetings. Meetings are how the pudding is made for a lot of business moms, so remember the time you need to invoice, funnel your future clients, and *allllll* the rest.

Another tip on effectively structuring your day in blocks is to put your low-hanging fruit last on the to-do list so it doesn't make its way to your calendar of priorities. You will often find a few minutes—say, if a call wraps early—in need of something mindless, which low-hanging fruit is great for. I am guilty of going for the easy stuff to slide into my day, but that can slip into hitting the elementary stuff all day and never getting into effective space. Focusing on bigger projects first will likely put you in harmony with your natural productive or creative time. For most of us, that is the morning hours (read *The Power of When*, by Michael Breus), but if you allocate that time to the effortless stuff, you'll be exchanging creative time for admin tasks that could be done anytime. Having said that, there is something magical about crossing something off the list to kickstart motivation, but I managed to still feel successful by checking those boxes at the end of the day when I was naturally less focused.

At first, this structuring was the last thing I wanted to do. I tend to prefer spontaneity and surprises, but the many different ways to prioritize the priorities usually led to overwhelm. Or the numerous surprise emails that would send me in different directions had me feeling less like a business owner and more like a first responder. Leaving open windows on the calendar felt great to the freestyler in me, but so did feeling productive when I was working in blocks. I eventually had to turn off email and social media because it was too easy to go find that article I heard about and share it with my followers, then be lost in social media for fifteen minutes. Once I started tracking my time, I learned that things took a lot longer to do and distractions will always, *always* come up. I switched tactic and suddenly my top five drivers of success from monthly goal setting or the day's priorities were getting the time they deserved. It was easy to forget when I was so wrapped up in the business that its success hinged solely *on* me, and I would need to block time *for* me so I could be my best business self. Usually, two half-days on the weekend (because as a shop girl, I was also spending time in the store either serving customers or supporting the staff in heavy demand periods) were my free moments and they were deliberate and enjoyed. During the week, I put "me" things on my calendar in a different color (including doctors' appointments, self-care, or time with friends) and could quickly see how unbalanced my life was any week. I also recognized the need to visually *see space* on the calendar, otherwise I would invariably lack spaciousness in my creativity or my overall joy. This is essentially looking at your week in pie or percentage form. More specifically, a delicious apple pie where not only does your slice size vary, but so does each forkful's texture and consistency. Business is simply not homogenous, even if you sell only one thing. You'll wear many hats, you'll have many ways to reach your customer at various intervals in their customer journey, and too easy is a whole week, whole month, whole year of the pie filled up with the experience but rarely involves that ice cream on top. That is to say, that cream of realizing you *are* the boss and you *can* prioritize yourself. And it is worth repeating that you *can* enjoy the whole *dessert*.

While your business might entirely hinge on you, remember you are not entirely jointed to your business, so allow me to emphasize again the importance of blocking time for mama maintenance (more on that in the next section). While you're working around the clock so you can make that dollar and feed your expanding belly, remember that if your business goes away, you're still you, so do make time to nourish you. You'll be a better business mom if you do.

There are a thousand time hacks out there but sometimes if your system allows, time works in your favor. In other words, if you let it, your inbox can even resolve things on its own in between productivity windows: Think about how much of your inbox is actually someone else's to-do list, whether it's someone asking for help (that they could perhaps find on their own) or someone getting something off their plate by putting it on yours. Sure, it needs your attention, but now that list is in competition with your own to-do list. When time is precious (and when isn't it?), experts agree that your inbox is the first thing that must go. You get to learn what it's like to triage your inbox and "CEO busy" the rest. Many experts say that if you let your inbox be your to-do list, you must delete/archive anything you aren't willing to deal with right in that moment. That is a bit of a stretch for me, but I do employ stars and "copy into calendar" or "copy into list" features to help me focus my inbox time on mission-critical things like advancing a contract. Emails confirming your mailing address for a vendor are solvable by a quick trip to your website, and anyone waiting can become resourceful and find said info. The habit of holding off on responding to email until end of day is empowering to the entrepreneur who feels like their time is not their own but of *all the things*. Sure, I check it on my phone in moments of technology weakness to make sure I am not needed for a quick response, but I know that either my project or my toddler deserves my best during the day, and emails requiring thoughtful responses are secondary to this moment. Besides, the email is rarely something that is advancing my career exponentially, or my ease, so it gets the least of my best moments.

So, how much is a good amount of time for priorities? To start, I liked to look back at my business plan to see which sections had the most ideas *or* the most hurdles and would visualize the pie accordingly. This then informed my time blocks for the week.

If I had some big gaps in getting to my financial projections, I'd start by giving that day more space—no lunch meetings or other priorities blocked on that day. I'd check in periodically on how that effort was panning out. Eventually I didn't use the plan to guide my energy, but it sure helped in the beginning to help me feel a little more connected with my dreams and how I chose to spend my time.

However, protecting time isn't entirely effective. Tasks will take a lot longer than you realize because when it's your baby, perfection rears its head. Blocking will help you avoid confusion and paralysis by perfectionism, *a little*.

Tracking time may seem like the last thing that matters in the early stages of starting a business. After all, you do actually need a business before you can start tracking its time. But what gets mea-

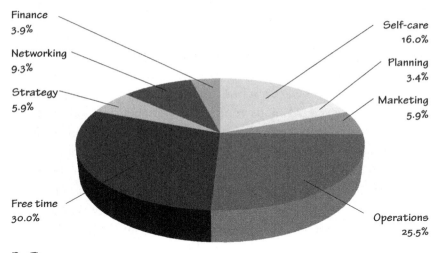

Finance
3.9%

Networking
9.3%

Strategy
5.9%

Free time
30.0%

Self-care
16.0%

Planning
3.4%

Marketing
5.9%

Operations
25.5%

Pro Tip
"Free time" isn't always free! Use this time to catch up on things you had to move down on your to-do list, do something for your sanity, or just call Grandma to see how she's doing!

sured gets improved, so it's worth the effort to manage this metric. This is especially true if you're starting a consulting business, where you really need to be in the habit of time tracking. It's easy: set up Toggl or, if upon research you could benefit from integration to invoicing or analytics, consider Harvest or Freckle. Tools like these keep you motivated but also let you see that when you've logged a ten-hour day, logging five the next is understandable. And encouraged. Most time trackers turn results into pie charts and voilà, a visual goal comparison. At the end of the week, look at your time and adjust accordingly for next week's goals. If, at the end of your 168 total hours each week, you only spent two wakeful hours recharging, perhaps that number becomes its own protected block the following week, to honor all that hard work. I suggest spending at least two of your waking hours every day) dedicated to charging those batteries. This can be reclaimed in four intervals:

- ▶ thirty-minute daily walk
- ▶ thirty minutes of eating or drinking (a cup of tea!) with intention
- ▶ getting up thirty minutes early to stretch and meditate
- ▶ disconnecting for thirty minutes of quiet time at bedtime

All done without a trip to the spa or having to really dedicate time on the calendar. For me, it wasn't so much about analyzing as it was awareness in looking up and realizing I spent twenty-five minutes on one scheduled post, and I needed to do the entire month's worth of postings in the next sixty-five minutes. When I looked at the amount of available time in the week, that slippage was coming out of personal time and nonworking hours. Up until that realization, I was acting as though time was fluid, when in reality, I was only borrowing from another bucket. Time does *not* grow on trees.

Both blocking and tracking keeps you on pace when you're overwhelmed and out of sight of the starting line. If you have fifty ways to approach some website user ideas and it happens to be Wednesday (for instance), start the timer and go; you'll be more effective for knowing you're on a clock. Your wheels won't spin as much. Your insights will increase. Your control factor will flourish. Still, try not to pay too much attention to the timer, or else it becomes a source of stress. If you can't focus or get in a groove that you can call productivity, stop the timer and do something else until you're able to let the timer work in your favor. Sometimes you need to keep the engine moving, especially when you can't possibly make another sales call but know you won't be back at this task again until some later window. This tactic also helps you become aware of possible tendencies to just scroll when you're having a hard time focusing. But if you can work in sprints (versus marathoning), this practice can help hone presence in life, relationships included. Strengthening focus for thirty minutes while working helps you practice being present and thus rewires the brain for more prolonged focus. The timer is revealing because it can help bring an awareness around some benign addictions and help start to manage them through interval training.

If the simple blocking and timing approach to productivity still isn't resonating, consider *why* the task matters, and see what unfolds. Did I ever fall in love with reconciling Quickbooks each month? No, but at least once a month I felt good about the service I was doing to my company's financial reports and also for the cash I was saving by not having my bookkeeper do this level of detail. I also felt good about the handle I had on our finances; in practice, the work became gratifying. As was the case for anything I wasn't trying to squeeze in between five meetings and two deliverables. Fewer wheels were spinning just getting by, picking up and putting down projects, and I was able to create more space to *create*.

Lastly, businesses are big. Too easily does the admin take over, and when 80 percent of your time is serving 20 percent of your business plan (the operations or admin), the results you strive for become improbable. Keep in mind that 20 percent of your energy *can* be spent on 80 percent of your returns, and that should help you make smarter choices in your business doings.

Systems for Sanity and Scalability

Time management is the first hierarchy of needs. After that, it's making sure you have systems to keep you organized (i.e., keeping track of the moving pieces and tasks that are too granular for calendar entries) and the details that go into the processes (like accepting inventory and pricing new stock, for instance). Time management is actually sanity management, and if your sanity isn't enough motivation, it's your baby's future health you're orchestrating here. For me, *how* to spend my time was the thing I spent a lotta time on. Wanting to scale the business from day one added this extra pressure. Then I reflected on how I sometimes wanted to relieve myself of the burden of deciding; I found structuring my time did help here. All this thinking and no ROI to justify it. I go into value as it pertains to rate setting in chapter

3, but for now, consider time as the only resource within your domain that has the highest return. One unit of time can quite possibly get you 1.5 units in return. Invest it well. Almost every aspect of startup land can have a time factor overlay, and it should. This is your time to work like mad to get this thing born. If there are ways to make it happen faster or with ease, do them! It could take you three times as long to build your own website (that looks like you did it for free) or you can make the investment, get it done for a few thousand dollars, and feel good about it because it was the most efficient thing you did today. Trading off other startup areas to score one for your time account is still a win in the bootstrapping category. Something that will take so much time and still not be amazing is not worth your time. Consider if it will get you the possible 1.5 units back if you do it yourself. *Probably not.* Efficiency is the name of the startup game. Even if you're the get-things-done type and figuring out how is totally in your nature, still reflect for a minute, to challenge your old habits and think like the person who is writing your story. Smart decisions aren't necessarily cheap decisions, but if you do it right the first time, it's still more economical (and less maniacal) in the long run. You're probably bootstrapping a thousand ways to Wednesday anyway.

A note on notes. Before figuring out my systems and organization, I got started with the first notetaking tool I heard of (Evernote), because it seemed pretty snazzy and everyone was using it. Except I couldn't get it to work when my iPad was offline at business meetings and ended up never using the cool features that I thought I'd enjoy, like handwriting notes and emailing. Being out of touch with my tool

---

Smart decisions aren't necessarily cheap decisions, but if you do it right the first time, it's still more economical (and less maniacal) in the long run.

---

meant I never went back to the notes besides pulling things into my to-do lists. My "notes" function on my phone quickly replaced the tool and worked perfectly for any notetaking I needed to do in meetings, and it also housed my rolling to-do list before things got put into my calendar to ensure execution. It replaced my stickies, was the basis of any future whiteboarding (ideas I needed to connect visually), and because it was visible on my computer, I could easily paste it into proposals or strategy documents. Basic but effective. But Evernote and other apps might work for you. Start by thinking about what matters to you or where you perceive pain points as you collect and manage information. Now imagine those processes when you're cooking with some gas and how quickly tedious tasks burn in flames. You may have to try a few strategies before honing yours, but I'd recommend three or four ways to manage yourself (this includes your to-do lists, calendar, and CRM and project management). If you have your priorities on your calendar, your details in a project management tool (like Asana, which I found when my to-do list was too large and I fell in love with for a million reasons including sorting and delegation), and a CRM like 17Hats to manage invoices and communications to customers, then you're done. With these three approaches, your main bases should be covered. Have a fun marketing idea? Don't sticky it; tag it to marketing in your virtual project manager tool and come back to it when you're ready to focus on marketing and execution. It doesn't get lost in a sea of notes, and you can visually see when the same idea keeps coming up. If you need to turn it into a to-do that gets put on your calendar—boom, you're automated. Even if you prefer the satisfaction of scratching things off a list, you may begin experiencing similar satiation by watching your list shrink electronically or by clicking a completion box instead. Whatever the technology, start with your list of what you need and don't delay with simplifying your business (and actual) life.

There's an app for everything in today's innovation economy, and there are many tools to bridge gaps untold, so even storage and file

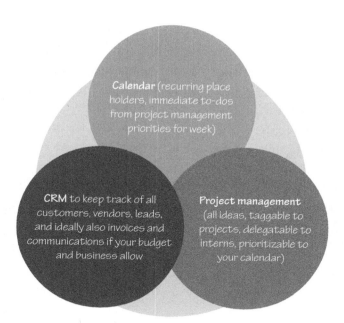

Calendar (recurring place holders, immediate to-dos from project management priorities for week)

CRM to keep track of all customers, vendors, leads, and ideally also invoices and communications if your budget and business allow

Project management (all ideas, taggable to projects, delegatable to interns, prioritizable to your calendar)

sharing will come with options. Consider the top three and make a decision that satisfies you now and the you in three years.

With business nesting in full effect with my newfound time and efficiency measures, I became selective about who I would meet with, selective about projects I'd open myself to because of resource constraints, and reflective of how each intersection would either lead me closer to or further from my goal. All this simply by being more intentional with the structure of my week and the systems I chose to keep me on track.

Notwithstanding the many timesaving systems for the larger functions of business outside of self-management, your "financials" house must be in order when you're merrily nesting the rest of your preparations. You don't have to solve for all of your future problems, but making money will absolutely be a part of your business, so get your tracking down before that money starts to flow. Like opening your wallet and gesturing that you're ready for business, invite that dollar by having a system to receive it, track it, allocate it, and honor it. Good structure here (read: not on a spreadsheet) will pay dividends down the road. The longer you wait to implement your bookkeeping tool, the harder it will be. Promise.

There's a recurrent theme in this book and it's not to quit your job too early. In this early nesting phase, with these internal shifts, it's good to have something steady (like your old job) to help ground you as the rest of your perspectives and approaches begin to change. Soon, it will be your systems that help keep you sane.

Undeniable Business Skill #6: Working Well-Being

Bosses of impossible obliviousness or bountiful bureaucracy often help entrepreneurs justify their exit into the blissful pasture of innovation and executive decisions. Yet, the evolved you will gently offer that dealing with tough personalities is a life problem, not simply a work problem, and there is a lot more work to working for yourself than anyone is willing to admit. With the abundance of work, responsibility, and isolation, the stakes are naturally higher, even if you're doing this thing the lean way. These attributes can make owning a business a lonely and possibly depressing adventure. The good and bad news is it all comes down to you. Learning more about yourself and developing a deep connection to your true talents (and developing areas) can broaden your viewscape. How you work with yourself is the most important aspect of inquiry because the adage is true: wherever you go, there you are. And *you* are what's sustaining this business . . . at least for now. Sustainability is defined broadly for business, but it always comes back to the vehicle (ahem) you that sees efforts through. So, you can come at this wildly or you can take a pregnant pause and think *you* through. *Time and time again.* Fret not, this learning is a rite of passage that can be used to your advantage. It is a baseline of knowing *you* can make a notable difference in *your* experience. Next, and oh so importantly, recognize how you interact with other personalities and temperaments to see more of the mechanics and less of the emotion in the interaction. It's worth the effort to know your tendencies, now magnified with you on top with no other props, to recognize how your personality interacts with others, and to develop strategies on how to handle it best. After all, you're fulfilling your purpose, so you might as well get comfortable with the *you* that's birthing this baby.

Preparing yourself for the obvious tasks is easy when stick-to-itiveness and excitement are working in your favor because it's *yours*. Preparing yourself to take no offense or to get back on the horse every time you're down is harder *because* it is yours. You don't have a choice.

You're doing it because you chose this . . . and it's beautiful. This is known as resilience training: understanding what it will take to be ready and to be successful and tweaking that understanding (i.e., practice trying) again and again. This is what meditation taught me, and I'm so glad I found it early in my journey. Everything will be in high contrast, fears will riptide, and onslaughts of surprises will either exhilarate or exterminate your sense of self. In both cases, the easiest thing to do is the worst: prioritizing your work and not your personal evolution, to just. get. by. And lost is the purpose path you set out to explore. Feeling and internalizing every bump in the road means increased risk of chronic stress. Chronic stress means an inability to remember or use your brain's executive functions (like planning and analyzing), and if you're in that extricated place, what was the point of going out on your own? It can and will be tough at times. Your lead investor or expected pool of customers may go silent. Your fears may actualize. But you will have prepared yourself; you'll be ready.

Tactics to Evolve and Strengthen Entrepreneurial Resiliency

Scenario	Heroine-in-Training Tactic
If you're stuck, out of creative juices, or recognizing that you're in low gear, trying to power through (for hours on end).	Stop! Don't push the issue. Go for a gratitude walk, go hang out with a BFF, go do laughter yoga. Do not look at your competitors or your to-do list. Powering through is precisely the sign that you need a break.
If you're faced with unknowns, regular setbacks, and signs that stakes are high.	Accept the stakes. Love them. Make the best decision you can make in this moment. Ask yourself: Is this going to matter in three days? Three months? This gets you back into the big picture and refocused.

Scenario	Heroine-in-Training Tactic
If you're experiencing impostor syndrome, a keen awareness that you don't know what you don't know, or conceding that you know zip about running a business.	Think of these as your reality checks. You're learning about grace. You're still learning about a thing everyone else thinks you're crushing. You're learning about patience . . . and cravings! Wanting to be the best but contending with having to learn, time and time again. Tip: fake it till you make it and focus on a healthy environment for baby to thrive. No one knows the answers . . . but you will. And you'll get to look back at those lessons and likely help another business mama along.
When you get to a point where you can't make another decision . . . like ordering dinner because you can't even put a protein with a vegetable. As fun as it is being boss, you'll get tired of being in charge, and you'll want someone else to guide you at times.	Get yourself a trainer in some other area of life (fitness or meditation podcasts come to mind). Let them take the reins for that category. Learn to let go of doubt—get comfortable making a decision and sticking to it (best decision for today's business isn't always the best choice for the future but accepting that if it comes up again, time will help inform the choice).
When you have a good freak-out (at least one) about the validity of your company. *Is this even worth it?!*	Pull out your business plan, the heart of this mission. Call your business BFFs. Spend at least two days doing nothing business and everything intention. Your motivation will remind you, and if adversity overcomes purpose, you'll recognize your path if you align with why you started this in the beginning.
When the day-to-day becomes more solitary. Even if working around other people, you're not in the same position or perspective as them . . . and it's lonely up there.	Like fully accepting how exhausting creating and birthing anything is, you'll never believe it till you're in it. Put regular love fests on your calendar. Pick three people who inspire you, love you, feel you, and see them monthly. Go ahead and put them on your calendar now. And if that's not enough, think about the end. Visualize why you're doing this, how this working independently funds your actual babies' college or puts you on boards you never imagined.

Scenario	Heroine-in-Training Tactic
When you feel overwhelmed and you don't even know where to start or what to prioritize.	Recognize that you only experience this sensation the first or second time you're faced with a problem. If it's hard, the next time will be easier, and you'll be prepared. You can also tackle overwhelm in terms of tasks. Try looking at the overall value you're providing the world through your customers' experience and decide which task matters more in that moment. You can't always avoid reconciling Quickbooks in the name of customer satisfaction, but you *can* agree to postpone the exercise to a time when your reserves of creative energy are low.
You're experiencing frustration or hardship because even though you have more autonomy, the answers aren't coming as fast as you'd like.	Say hello to your Buddha business, here to teach you how to begin again. And again. And again. Be patient and kind to yourself. A setback can sometimes be a good thing: it could be life cleaning something out in order to make room for something better. Call on your own strengths: How have you picked yourself up from a problem client/issue in the workplace already? Sometimes you have to reel it back in to cast again. And that's life. No signs of failure per se. You get to choose if these delays or surprises are worth the internalization or not.

How you let these monologues affect your psyche or your journey is a function of your resilience, which is to say, how high your emotional quotient (EQ) is as an entrepreneur. EQ is loosely defined as a person's ability to have an awareness of emotions and their level of empathy in dealing with others, measured in numerical form. When wearing the big decision-making hats of the C suite, emotional intelligence is called on ceaselessly. And strengthening the EQ is absolutely something that is done *only* in difficulty, so look at those moments lovingly; they are here to evolve you. While in the early stages, nurture a higher EQ by

▶ pacing yourself.
▶ serving your needs mentally, physically, and financially. Note that this will be the resource that is likely most strained/needs

the most love from either spending more than you expected, things taking longer than expected, or not appreciating business cycles or slow seasons. Practice your long game and trust yourself.

▶ reminding yourself that everything you're doing is for a purpose. You have taken the time to evaluate if what you're doing is a priority or aligned with your plan—which *screams* purpose. Right!?

▶ practicing leaning on a close confidante or business guru who can sounding-board or guide when you're overwhelmed. It can be very lonely in your head, and talking things through with someone who can offer sound advice is necessary, so figure out who is with you for the long haul and who can remind you what you're capable of.

▶ practicing detachment. Isolating the issues and getting to constructive areas is something you'll need to do regularly, so practicing detachment will help your emotions stay balanced and your EQ sharp.

Another sanity support is to have a plan B for anything that's uncertain (like financing), to help you feel like you're still on a path even in the very likely event that things don't go according to your hopes. Plan B may be only launching half of your product line or pushing out hiring staff . . . or it could mean finding a partner or moonlighting with your day job a little longer. For sanity's sake, learn to love those options, even if they are not your preferred choice.

You can embrace these options even before you launch. You can choose not to quit your day job, because despite the annoyances, you're doing it for a good reason. Quit when there's so much momentum around your business that you *need* to reclaim those day-job hours to achieve more in your business. *In other words, when the day job is standing in the way of your success, then you'll know it's time, and those are the feels you are after.* Being the best parent might require you to make sacrifices that aren't ideal, but learning to appreciate the alternative path can help you feel more resilient in the face of other surprises. Like it or not, the next wave is coming.

Real resiliency. I spend a lot of time with clients managing their expectations because of what it can do to their mental peace. Entrepreneurs are naturally optimistic, and that can get them into trouble when things don't go according to hope or plan. Get a good meditation app: it takes three minutes a day and you can watch how your response to these tests changes. I find myself now asking How am I doing with this test? when my emotions start moving, a new awareness that wasn't a part of my experience in the beginning.

I've talked about this evolved perspective relative to your business skill set, but a deeper look is prudent. To get to know your tendencies, first think about taking a few current assessments (like the Keirsey Temperament Sorter or the Clifton Strengths Finder). These can reveal a lot about you, quickly generating contra practices to help retrain the brain, as your understanding of yourself, then of others, increases. For instance, if you're the Overachieving Perfectionist, one practice to adopt is to remember to be patient and kind with yourself. A helpful mantra could be "done is better than perfect." If you're a respectful, wait-to-be-called-on person, you'll benefit from telling yourself out loud how confident you've become now that you're in the driver's seat, and that you will need to be more verbal with your needs if your business is to prosper. If that's you, also consider reading Jen Sincero's *You Are a Badass.* I was all kinds of comfortable with my Myers–Briggs assessment while I was a corporate person, but the moment I started working outside of the constructs of "shoulds" here in the entrepreneurial world (people *should* respond within twenty-four hours; I *should* be able to find the answer to this; they *should* want my business . . .), I realized I needed to get my ego in check before I let the outside world affect the champion inside. I needed to know the true me in a categorical sense to then build a net to catch the super dream chaser when she started to navigate uncomfortable territory (which was a lot!). When I realized that I am a Connected, Futuristic, belief-driven Relator and Activator (from the Clifton Strengths Finder), I validated what I suspected but then gave myself permission to truly own the following:

- I rely heavily on the Universe to guide me. That, and I am quite prone to start things. This meant that if I don't check myself, I can find meaning in everyone or thing I come upon and before I know it, I'm starting three new businesses while my last business still needs some serious strategy execution. *Guilt blush.*

- I can look past complexities and think I can figure things out. *Loosens shirt collar.*

- If all that is true, I should be partnering with a subject matter expert to accomplish big programs, versus someone I like a lot and is probably a lot like me. *Painful accepting gulp.*

Truth be told, I kind of already knew these traits about myself. What hit home was to value and appreciate the characteristics and see how impactful they actually were. Also, understanding my own temperament helped me understand how I interact with *other* temperaments. For instance, being characterized as "futuristic" means that while I do like to look at the horizon, if I'm peering too far, ideas become vague and I will likely have a hard time articulating a value proposition that may be difficult for an external party to appreciate. And let's face it, when you're open for business, other people are all you have. No business exists without sales, and no sales transaction is generated without some sort of interaction, unless you are selling stocks or cryptocurrency. Said differently, relationships can define your entrepreneurial experience, including your relationship with yourself. This increased awareness can create an opportunity for a high-caliber exchange, especially when faced with a difficult or stressful interaction. Questions like *Are they growing by this action? Are they expanding their impact by inaction? Does that align with the person they believe themselves to be? Do their reactions follow suit with who they ground in when time or demands allow? Does this work with the businessperson I am?* These can make that interaction deeper and less emotional at the same time. I know I am a different mom to my children when I'm more firmly rooted in the person I believe I am. Imagine if everyone tuned in to their tendencies, loved them up, and reflected that acceptance to the world. Our careers, commutes, and cravings would feel completely different.

Just like a human mom-to-be needs to strengthen her core and support her mental health, it's similarly critical to begin a practice now to help sustain you through the long nights and exciting times as well as the disappointments that inevitably will be peppered in. Entrepreneurship is synonymous with *decisions.* Choosing your overall worldview—your self-view—is the most important decision. It's how you'll face the world. Choosing to prioritize a practice that helps with your perspective will be beneficial to your business relationships. Getting caught up in statistics is one way to lose perspective and is often unimportant to the mission of your business, yet data is all you can rely on. This is an example of how your day-to-day experience can influence your overall business experience and long-term sustainability. These practices, evolutions, and adjustments are the signs of life, and are needed to create a healthy environment for this beautiful entity you're about to birth.

Before moving to the tactical skills of feeding, marketing, and financing your baby-to-be, take a moment to reflect on the softer skills that make you a good mama. And smile at those early adaptations. You're spiritually becoming the business mom you were meant to be. Then, moving into preparing yourself emotionally, it's healthy to put some details into that timeline you've certainly begun developing. Consider how you'll integrate these softer nuances, as well as bracing yourself with the more global, business-imperative understandings laid out in the next chapter. When building your timeline, mark your delivery (target) date and back into it. If you're opening a retail store-front, allow more time for the pieces (like lawyers, real estate agents, bankers, and contractors) that are out of your control. It's healthy to have the goal in sight, so go ahead and create a realistic timeline. We'll fill in the details as we go along.

Expecting: Adaptations

It's all changing, even the skills you thought you were strong in, because you've never operated in this context before. Recognize the importance of the skill to the ease of your business and think about the learning curve in relation to a healthy timeline.

▶ If you need a refresher, consider the TED Talks and Media Favorites cited at the end in the resources appendix.
▶ Your relationship to yourself is changing, and new relationships will only complicate matters. Get to know yourself super well.
▶ Time management really needs to work for you. It's important to remember that you're essentially the project manager of a lean startup of at least five employees (the five hats you'll wear: CEO, CFO, CMO, COO, and CTO). With some conscious effort, you'll find systems that work for you. And habits around this topic do matter. What you do daily creates your business, and something that has the potential to make you more efficient, like letting go of your paper calendar, might evolve you to more effective heights.
▶ For resiliency training, connect to yourself via meditation and with your innate talents and strengths via recognized tools mentioned within this chapter.

☐ Your Readiness Journal

Sketch here what you'll need from your networking experience. This is your networking strategy sketch. It may sound like overkill, but a five-*minute* intention exercise can save you five *hours* of wasted networking time. List out the personalities and the professions you'll want to meet initially. Imagine who is on your future board and the types of venues where you are most likely to find those relationships.

_____

_____

_____

_____

_____

_____

_____

_____

Reflect back on your dreamed timeline in chapter 1. Now that you've embraced some additional timeline elements, what has changed?

3

Business Planning
and Roadmapping

Expect Plans for Your Plans

You know that feeling when you wish you had prepared a little more for the interview or perhaps done a bit of research on the hotel you booked for the one vacation you took this year? The rapid surge of guilt-fueled fear just because you could have planned a smidge more and not had any of the stress hormone cortisol pulsing through your blood? Well the cortisol will come, but we don't need to create extra emotions around the experience of not having prepared. The difference with a business is that you get to take the poor planning memories and put them in a jar and shake it up to get the biggest leap of your lifetime, possibly with all of your resources at stake. Plan. And if you read nothing else in this first-timers' guide, PLAN EARLY. The creation of my concept occurred right alongside the business planning process, and I would recommend no different for any first-time moms. Getting carried away with ideas without some feasibility analysis to temper plans or check the "idea overwhelm" is almost *too* easy for women who are mostly wired for delivery and the details therein. If you haven't already put some concrete analysis around your concept, today is the day to assess every variable in your business model. And if you do have some basic plans in place, this chapter will help you gauge your timing and readiness by evaluating all the questions you can ask yourself while preparing for what can be a monumental risk (with exponential rewards, if calculated correctly).

If you've had children, you know the situation: your go bag is packed, car seat installed, and the family is on call for taking care of the pets. *Everything should be in place.* But your soul is in full-on panic because the endgame, it turns out, is a very different sport. Arming yourself with theoretical answers to probable questions and orienting yourself with a prepared mindset is the goal. Of course, you can over-plan to the point where you need to execute, but if done purposefully, planning is a process that can be shortcut in future pivots or business creations as a result of having embodied the questions that come up during the initial planning process.

Readiness is not just the financial preparedness and backup planning to keep you fed while you're putting together the foundation. It's having a good plan and network *and* a long-range view for maintenance and future phases of execution. The goal is simply to be as prepared as a new business mom can be for the first few years, with the eye on making your prodigy the best version of themselves come adulthood. *Enter the all-mighty, peace-bearing business plan, and its sanity sister, the strategic plan.* Prepared in the business sense means putting your heart where your head is in the preannouncement phase and now putting your head where your money is going to be spent. Two baby steps. No one is expecting you to be an expert as soon as the baby business is here. Every mom would agree it's mostly on-the-job learning with a few how-to diaper/feed primers and some general plans to prop you up in the early stages. Formal plan or not, sleepless nights will happen and you'll need to draw on your preparedness to help you function later, when business life gets real. This chapter introduces the important tactical elements that must be in place in order for you to feel confident about what the business is capable of. The business bones are starting to form, and it is time to ensure the skeletal system is going to support the baby business of your dreams.

A Quick Note on Legal Structures

Most startups are LLCs or sole proprietorships, with how much protection you need and what tax treatment you prefer being primary variables. Interview a few accountants and get their take as you make your decision about partnering with them. Do some research on the top five deductions for self-employed individuals so you have an opinion before seeking advice on structuring your entity. No free advice can be binding, and this particular election can be changed later if your business evolves or you find another structure. The fee for creating an LLC varies by state; some business-friendly states are as low as $50 with $10 renewals; others charge as much as $500 annually.

The sooner you register your business, the faster you'll secure your name, and if there is ever a copycat question, at least you'll have that much on file. If you're certain of the name, there's no harm in registering it (taxes only begin when you set up your tax accounts). An important thing to note is that registering your business name doesn't protect it from being used in other states, so consider if trademarking makes sense once you have examples of using the name in conjunction with your product or specialized service.

Timeline Tip

Concise. While it's important to keep your business plan succinct by not including every single idea you have, now is the best time to think through all your ideas, how details will play into costs, returns on time/energy investment, and what will ultimately be prioritized versus left out of the strategic plan. Remember, the business planning process is a means to help you slow down and intentionally build the bones of your baby business. Some argue that *doing* is more important than thinking or planning when you need to get your concept out into the world and start adjusting for feedback. I don't disagree with that philosophy when inaction is costing more than the business can afford. But a proper ounce of planning is worth a pound of course correction. If thoughtfully organizing the elements of a business in one place isn't reason enough, please allow me to convince you of the importance of the business planning exercise, especially for your first baby business.

▶ Every business studied in B school has a business plan. Yours should be no exception.

▶ By having a script, you can focus your energy; and having a sense of progress will help your sanity as you enter unchartered territory.

▶ With this mental space, you may take on new opportunities to see what is possible and in alignment with your mission.

▶ Your determination and perseverance will benefit from knowing you thought holistically through as many scenarios and opportunities as possible, later when you wax and wane between exhaustion and exhilaration.

▶ Your timeline will be ready for any banker, investor, or occasional vendor . . . and they'll know you're legit.

▶ Your dreamer tendency could stand to have a moment of not plowing ahead and instead dedicate a week of research and thought organization to your cause.

- This baby business is potentially the biggest thing you've ever created, and you deserve to feel the depths of this terrific shift.

Going through the detailed exercise of putting every aspect of your business onto paper may seem tedious and unnecessary right now, when all you want to do is just create or do. But it can be a healthy focal point when new ideas or suggestions come that may not align with your intended direction, or may distract you from what matters, or may require additional resources to truly do the right way. So in this respect, think of your business plan as your high-level project plan. Put the fundamentals in first and then build from there. The plan is your structure and your engine. The business will evolve away from the plan, and that's totally fine as long as it is an intentional, healthy pivot. I let my business evolve naturally and twelve months in was doing things that had never occurred to me, like private events, rotating food menu, and offsite talks; but at each opportunity, I always glanced back at the business plan to see if this detracted from anything else I wanted to achieve in the first year. If it was still worth it, I made sure to manage my expectations of other areas. For instance, rather than focusing on the online store revenue stream, I shifted to develop new catering options for events (to help with supply chain, customer preferences, and efficiencies at the event) to fully service the new and huge revenue stream. The trade-off was that I was also creating corresponding point-of-sale (POS) buttons, par/reorder parameters, and protocols for invoicing; managing deposits; closing down the store to regular customers; using the opportunity as marketing to event attendees; and ensuring the event was staffed for a smooth experience, because customers paid a premium to rent our space. The margins were greater for events than for the online store, and a quick assessment of up-front costs helped me confidently decide that the online store was not a priority at that time. It was a beautiful pivot that netted us much more than investing time and resources into promoting our online store, and it was a healthy evolution that made sense *after* reflecting on the plan I painstakingly created.

Expect Simplicity

It's so easy, especially in the first few years as you're still figuring what works or what doesn't, to try anything to get your name out and be responsive to every single customer's requests. My friend has an online T-shirt company with a specific mission and a product people love. But in the beginning, she let her customers guide her color choices and styles of neckline so much that she ended up with a ton of inventory that was compelling to only a few. Even though it seemed like her business was evolving away from multiple options in support of a specific theme with many variations, because the feedback was to expand the colors and not the shirt design, once customers bought their shirt, they had their bold color and didn't want other bold colors of the same design, after all.

By focusing on what was planned for (six new designs a year in the case of my friend's shirt company), there's a sense of control over what needs to be done to go to market. If it's working, don't change anything, but rather wait a few months and plan to layer in some innovative revenue streams to reach a *new* segment, or at very minimum, build on the needs of existing clientele. By complicating your offering, you can choke your cash flow if an attempt at diversification goes south, and even appear disjointed if you're responding to feedback that isn't in line with your goal or brand. It's difficult when you're in the moment, but practicing some discernment before casting a reactive wide net is important.

Application to Business

Simple saves. Only diversify beyond planned revenue streams in the early days if you can see the impact in your numbers *and* it comes with little effort. If you're planning to try something new after only a few months, consider how long your product or offering really needs to infiltrate the market. Consider other channels to reach your market instead of starting over with an additional product or service to sell. When setting up your plan, try to have more than one but fewer than five revenue streams, to keep your operations simple in the first year or so. You have so much to learn, and each revenue stream comes with many variables and ways to reach the customer, so don't overcomplicate things until you can handle trying out something new. In hindsight, my friend could have easily decided to take the best suggestions at the end the first year, but she got carried away in the feels of having a following that she wanted to thank by responding to their ideas. In addition to not being able to move product, she ended up having to do a lot of work to get pictures online of the different colors/styles to help sell the product, and had to quickly upgrade her inventory system because her number of SKUs more than quadrupled. It also took her away from what she set out to do, which was to create products that resonated with a certain group of people. She fell into the validation trap (discussed more in chapter 4). Worst of all, her innovation was stymied and she quickly found herself working for a business that she didn't recognize or enjoy with the added administrative burden. She still recovered, but it's a great example of how relevant the plan can be once the baby is here and you're getting a whole lot of advice.

Plans come in various shapes and sizes, from the one-pager (or business model canvas) to the full-on thirty pages of well-depicted details. No matter the format, you'll need to spend time crunching numbers and deepening your belief in your mission and the returns on all your efforts. What goes into the plan can also be dictated by who is looking at it. Writing the full-blown plan requires a few weeks of modeling and answering some key questions that most bankers, real estate agents, and investors will want to know. If you will need traditional business financing, it's worth going through the effort of the full-length plan, to be ready for them. Appendix 1 (page 249) has details of what's needed. If only you and your partner will see the details of the business, you might be able to get by with a one-pager, but do not shortcut the research and the inputs. The answers to these four questions should be in all plans.

1   *Who* is your customer (and buying patterns)?
2   *What* is your market (and competitors)?
3   *How* will you market in light of #1 and #2?
4   *How* will you make money, in light of #1, 2, and 3; and *when* will you break even/what margin will be available to fund growth?

Put real data behind these questions and do not lie to yourself or sugarcoat the outcomes. I say this for the sake of your sanity, however it's widely known that numbers are, well, fluffy in the projection phase and it's really hard to achieve accuracy. Not that they asked for my advice, but Ben and Jerry's founders took a different approach and it still worked out (but not without heartache, which is what I'm hoping to minimize for you, mama). Ben Cohen and Jerry Greenfield didn't like their numbers, so they changed them. Yes, they fully admitted that with the loan they wanted and the growth they desired, their calculations simply would not do. So they set new numbers and the fairy ice cream godmothers stood by in the wings of Vermont. It worked out for them. While this is a wonderful Cinderella story, you will do yourself no favors by being overly optimistic about your data in the planning phase. Save that for when it looks good on paper but you're still trying to connect the rest of the dots. In connecting the dots, think about any unanswered questions your concept presents, because anyone who will care about you or your business (spouse, investors, etc.) will look for the care you put into this document, ensuring that you thought through everything, including peering into the future for trends or opportunities or uncertainties. Does this sound daunting to someone who has never done it? It should, except you're a risk taker with entrepreneur wiring, so you've totally got this step.

Even if you're the only person who will be reviewing the business plan, it's a chance to put details to your dreams and make sure you've thought about ev-er-y-thing you could possibly do to attract revenue and in turn, rank those ideas in terms of biggest return and biggest priority. They're all good ideas when you don't know how the market will respond, so you have to start somewhere and not try to do it all.

Before sketching your plan, first pause, set your intention on doing this to the best of your ability, and orient with the goal before getting carried away in what this business can do.

First and foremost, the goal is to serve a purpose. Was it to create financial freedom for you? Whether it be details for a company meant to fill a gap in the marketplace while the kids are at school or a technology solution that will virtually save lives, before embarking on planning, remind yourself of the goal. Then move to marketing—the ideas and vehicles that will get to the goal. Next, planning will involve how much your ideas will cost and how much you can expect to see in return. The final bit of planning is strategizing the operational and nuanced elements that will make the business function. All three pictures will light your way and make all the things possible.

Step 1: Start with Marketing

Specifically, start with each of your products or service offerings. These are your primary revenue streams. Ask yourself if there are various ways you can sell the same thing to many people, for example an online store, at trade shows, or wholesale. Think about the product in the hands of your customer and how it got there. Imagine what the buyer looks like (really imagine her, in detail!) because from there, you'll figure out where they are/how you'll reach them. It's that simple: who you are, who your customer is, and what language they speak (socially speaking, unless your business is an international import/export business, of course).

Consider using a whiteboard or an electronic sketch pad to tap into your right brain as you think creatively about your marketing makeup, or use the space here.

Knowing you means articulating your unique position in the marketplace. How your business can solve problems . . . differently. How you might even be solving a problem no one realized they had until they had you at their service. Consider yourself: why you're doing this, what unique perspective you bring, and why you are the right person for the job. These help connect you closer to your customer. It also helps to think long and hard about your brand. Your brand will define your thinking. It will help you say yes enthusiastically to opportunities that make sense and strengthen your business bond so well that if something doesn't resonate, you know it's because you have a clear brand. The brand is the look and tone of your business—are you playful, relaxed, sophisticated, energetic, indulgent, and accessible? Think of words that describe your brand and make sure you're prepared to reflect it in your collateral and blog writing.

_____

_____

_____

_____

_____

_____

_____

_____

Your logo and color schemes should reflect all of it (in other words, you probably won't use a combination of loud colors and a whimsical font if you're indicating you're a luxury business). One thing I learned long ago at a lecture on personal brand but rings true for a business brand is that "if it distracts, it detracts," so keep that in mind when deciding what represents you even before you open your mouth about your baby. I kept this in mind with the tea shop: the website looked and felt just as you'd expect to feel in the store. If it was too busy, it wasn't aligned with the word *harmony*, which I had chosen to help visualize the experience of the brand.

Knowing you also helps you narrow in on a price that reflects your value *and* position in the marketplace. Being true to your *why* will help you clearly navigate. And with that energy, consciously invite flow—that gorgeous resounding echo that doing your purpose can bring when you align with your passions and put some loving energy behind it. You know you, and you know what I'm talking about.

Knowing your customer means doing the research. Once your business is established, you can use things like Google Analytics to figure out who is visiting your page and what their preferences are, but in the beginning, you'll be narrowing the scope on your own. You can't possibly reach everyone, so better to refine your scope early on and possibly have a year two list or even a tiered list, provided you reach certain milestones. There are literally thousands of ways to reach one segment of the market, so face in a direction that checks with your intuition and your market research, and course correct when you need to. This is the beginning of many times you'll need to point yourself in a thoughtful direction and go.

Knowing your customer also means thinking about who will pay for your offering (hopefully time and time again). If you're selling expensive wedding invitations, your customer might be referrals from more affluent customers (and perhaps not necessarily your friends or peers). Think about what matters to the person who is shelling out money for your offering. Is it hard earned and is it an investment in her betterment or her happiness? Does she like the colors in your brand palette? In understanding your customer, by nature you're learning the market and can therefore conduct your marketing analysis. You can organize however it makes sense to your business, but textbooks suggest you can analyze a market by

- ▶ location
- ▶ population (gender/age)
- ▶ personality (opinions or lifestyles)
- ▶ behavior (purchasing patterns)
- ▶ income (this will affect the price you can actually charge)

I started by figuring out what percentage of the marketplace had disposable income (I needed to charge nearly $4.50 for a cup of tea in my high-cost real estate area), was into natural health (so much of my offering was to connect us closer to natural/ancient offerings of tea, herbs, foot soaks, reflexology), and what that person did for leisure or with their money. We'll go into marketing research a bit later, but I found a lot of this info at the library down the street. Determining what price is compelling to them (note the difference between the price you want in setting your value) helps define the marketing mix (the 4 P's: product, price, placement, and promotion) and communicates the competitive advantage in your market segment. This is where you can begin to translate your sketch into a documented business plan.

Knowing your customer's language means understanding where they spend their time (social media, playgroups, travel/things to do, meetups). Regular, direct contact will make your customers return, so build some sort of engagement into your marketing plan. It's not just about publishing content that is interesting to them; you also need to have bandwidth to respond to the tweets or Instagram followers to remind them there's a real person behind the business they've expressed an interest in. Feedback from your customer will be the biggest driver of your marketing strategy, so staying close to how they communicate will be an important rhythm to get into. If they tend more toward Instagram and less to email, you might invest more resources into that vehicle than your monthly newsletter. If a loyal local customer has told you they want to make it their personal mission to keep you in business, make sure you're catering to their messages of loving local.

(Very Early) Business Plan

Self	Customers	Marketing
▶ What perspective do I bring? ▶ Do my logo and color scheme match my brand? ▶ What is my why?	▶ Who is my potential customer? ▶ What does my potential customer look like? ▶ Where does my potential customer live? ▶ What is my potential customer willing to pay?	▶ What's the best way to reach my customer? ▶ What's the best use of social media to reach customers? ▶ How do I continue to engage once I establish contact?

All about that pricing. The most important way to price is to do so in a way that you're still relevant to your customer. Relevant so they get you and why you should be of interest to them. It also speaks to nurturing that interest over into importance, such that they have an internal pull or motivation to help you, refer business to you, and put their own name/recommendation on the line. If they've heard good things about you, they'll likely recommend you even before trying you. If you check their boxes for the type of brand they like to invest in, it's easy for them to relate to you. If you're consistent in maintaining your relationship with them (not in a pushy way), they'll be pleased to see your monthly updates and maybe even forward them along to their friends. *That kind of relevant.* Gary Vaynerchuck's *The Thank You Economy* illustrates the way to be relevant is about getting future customers to wish they were your customers. This means putting some serious resources around being a trusted friend to your potential customers. And, if you must price outside of the market, it's even more important to join conversations to *prove your potential* to potential customers. This could look like setting up search mentions on Twitter to answer certain questions of the day you'd like to help solve. Of course, this is only appropriate if it's done in a sincere way that introduces thoughts that are helpful to the conversation or overall industry, for instance, not an annoying approach that promotes only your business. This is how to make people care. They don't talk about things they don't care about. And getting them to care starts with caring for them first. Offer them knowledge and content that's helpful so they want to thank you by following, then sharing, and ultimately buying from you because you invested in them. This is your best customer anyway; someone who is already invested in you is so much easier to work with and to satisfy. If your business is more face to face, think about this currency when networking and when hiring employees. Are they mission loving, customer service driven, and can they keep the "conversation" and feeling of gratitude flowing on your behalf? It will buy your brand a lot to attract customers and employees who can relate and thus touch and feel the relevance to your business.

Social media is often included in promotion, but public relations–style promotion (PR) is a costlier option that may not align with a bootstrapped budget. You could either find someone who can barter with you who already runs a PR firm or get comfortable stalking local personalities or lifestyle bloggers (for instance) who can put in a good word for you. Note that both of these make a living from people paying for this service, so while you may get lucky and find someone willing to root for you, know that they aren't free. If they're doing it for free, you should find some meaningful way to thank them. Before I even had a soft launch, the local news blog reporter had scanned the county's permit applications and found that a unique concept was coming to the area. Their article was picked up by a food columnist for the *Washington Post* who then inspired a local columnist in *Arlington Magazine* to come do a feature. It was indeed synchronicity. These interviews occurred in the month between my soft launch and my grand opening, which was a tremendous stroke of luck for my outreach plan. I ultimately did meet a customer who was a PR professional who was willing to offer me some spots in some trade magazines and newsletters in exchange for some reflexology, but to get her to work the big outlets would require some time (and money) that I didn't have, so I worked with what I had. Those articles did spur some additional interviews and upped our website hits and SEO, so it was a win. In later years, I had a store manager who wanted to get into PR ultimately who did a lot of the blogger/reporter/publication stalking for us. We didn't see a lot of luck on our own, but we did see enough to validate that if you need a public relations boost, work that into your marketing plan. One last point on public outreach: press releases can boost your promotion if timed well. For our actual grand opening, I released to the area news blogs and local papers, and it was mildly fruitful (had a very small write-up in one paper). Potentially that was because the word was already getting out (due to the afore-mentioned features) and the editor didn't see it as that newsworthy, or more likely, because it required some follow-up that I didn't have time for. I'm sure I could have seen bigger returns if I'd understood best timing, contacts, and outlets, but I didn't because I was about to have a business. The tea shop's launch party was a sell out, so it worked out, but I do see the utility in hiring a professional since you have one chance to time PR right.

Real-Life Example

If you haven't yet done so, read Miki Agrawal's *Do Cool Sh*t*, where she took on the role of PR herself and sent empty pizza boxes to relevant reporters and food columnists in New York City. Talk about hustling. She was creating an organic pizza shop in New York (the first of its kind in a sea of other perfectly good pizza shops). Simply opening up her disruptive pizza shop wouldn't be enough to get the splash she needed to make her model work, so she hit the media outlets with something bigger than a memo. The empty pizza boxes were meant to be a real invitation to the food editors to come see for themselves. And as if the pizza box wasn't enough, many of the buildings were highly secured, and to get the boxes delivered, she had to go through some serious measures simply to get their attention. She did it all herself (on her bike riding around Manhattan). She was relentless and followed up with everyone leading up to the day of the launch, as good PR approaches do. It seemed like such an effort (beyond a full-time commitment) but it was worth it, and she made the splash she needed.

Now, with lots of thoughts stirring, take a good pregnant pause and sketch out the marketing components of your business plan, keeping your demographic, how you'll differentiate, and how you'll create value by investing in your customer firmly in mind. Then, to be truly thoughtful, get comfortable with the industry and take note of the landscape in your plan with the resources outlined in this section.

Pro Tip

In formal plans, avoid illustrating that you're the only person in the marketplace. First, because you need to be honest with yourself! Even if no one else is doing what you hope to do, there are still thousands of other ways people could spend their money. Second, if you're looking for investors or lenders, they want to know examples of where this is happening elsewhere. Competition is good: It validates the market and shows you can compete here. Essentially, an attractive business has competitors but also has a differentiation plan and unique competitive advantages to make the endeavor probable and sustainable.

Factors that may help you craft your advantage include price, quality, location, reputation (easy to say, hard to plan out), or any other unique attribute or knowledge you and your company offer. And even

Summary Marketing Plan*

Market analysis (who)	Marketing strategy (how)
Stats ▶ B2C ▶ Market size: 200,000 ▶ Total market demand: 2,000	**Four P's (engaging with and building trust with each segment):** **Product** ▶ Segments 1, 3, 4: in store ▶ Segment 2: mobile hugs
Market segments that you will target (why) 1 Moms needing care 2 Elderly needing love 3 Kids needing security 4 Couples needing quiet	**Price** ▶ $10 per hour, $100 unlimited in store ▶ $40 per hour, mobile hug **Promotion (first year)** ▶ Social media ▶ Fairs ▶ Radio shows
Target market characteristics ▶ Demographics: mid income, ages 8–80 ▶ Psychographics (attitudes and beliefs): believe we are social creatures needing healing touch ▶ Geographics: willling to drive 10 minutes ▶ Behavioral characteristics: willing to prioritize mental health ▶ Needs and wants (their hierarchy of needs that you can speak to): wellness and companionship	**Placement** Class B real estate **Engagement (how)** High-quality experience that makes everyone feel safer and more loved than before the transaction **Competition (who or what they are, how they compare in size and volume, their advantages and disadvantages, how they are distinguished):** ▶ Antidepressants ▶ Therapists **Brand pillars (what you stand for)** Safe, secure, professional, willing to embrace mental health

* This is not the tactical plan but a summary of who you'll reach and generally how

if your advantage is easily defined today, still contemplate how long you can assume that position. Eventually there will be copycats and you'll need to either change your approach or find ways to maintain your advantage and stay competitive. Here are some tools to assess the industry you're entering and conduct an analysis on your competitive advantage (how you will do it differently):

- Looking for information on industries? Try www.bizstats. com to figure out how money is spent in a particular industry.
- If you're curious what industry leaders are fetching in their part of the market, look to http://finance.yahoo.com, which also offers general industry info (the landscape).
- Visit www.census.gov (American factfinder) to drill down on certain geographic areas.
- If you're planning to reach customers in person or have a physical pop-up, www.zipskinny.com has detailed profiles of market by zip code.
- Chamber of Commerce sites often offer local demographics (go to info/biz support services even if you're a nonmember).
- www.claritas.com offers great information on market segmentation and a map to illustrate demographics, geographics, psychographics (how people act), and buying patterns in specific areas. Another psychographic site is www.quirks.com/topics/psychographics.

Even if you're not opening a storefront but you have an online store, it helps to see who is in your immediate area so you can go to vendor fairs, pop-ups, talks, and other face-to-face outreaches in order to gain some loyal customers the old-fashioned way. If you sell a product, consider locally owned stores whose owners might be willing to retail your product, or, if you want to put a display of brochures for your service business, which ones may be excited to tell their customers about you. All of these come with some level of data intelligence.

Don't forget the resources at your local library. Specifically, you can usually find access to referenceUSA, Business Insights journals, OneFile, newspapers, Ellyn, and Business Decision all in one place. Information like industry overviews and trade news, industry size or trends, competitors, and consumer spending or demographic info are invaluable and wholly worth taking the time to leverage these tools if your library has access to them.

While researching the marketplace and competition, allow me to offer a word of caution: If you've read *Blue Ocean Strategy*, you'll know that competition isn't benchmarking against other businesses, it's reaching customers in a new field that expands the market and creates new demand. The tea shop I created did have competitors (all coffee shops sell tea), and plenty of big chain loose leaf tea retail stores were showing up. None of them, however, were selling an experience and quenching a desperate and often unrecognized desire the population of the entire area had: to relax *while* they were already doing life. I mean pausing while living: meeting with friends, finishing their manuscript, having lunch, all of it can be done in a way that's accessible and can help them be better people for having taken a gentle moment in their day. For me, I anticipated their needs before they realized how much they'd enjoy the offering. And for you, just remember to know the special sauce that makes you different and customers reaching for you.

Another truth: while marketing is location, location, location (you can't create traffic if you're on an island at the far end of town), you can still create a flow of customers if you're positioned in a semi-attractive location by figuring out your before-and-after customer stops (yoga studio before visiting the tea shop, for instance). My shop was in an older part of town that had a hodgepodge of businesses, some relevant, some not. A yoga studio was obvious; less natural but still possible was a relationship with the hardware store across the street. Maybe my normal customer wasn't there (it may not come as a surprise that a large but not entire portion of my demographic was women), but their husbands and kids were and remembered me when it was time for holiday gifts, so I was sure to leave coupons at the hardware store as well. There was a dealership nearby, so regularly I delivered tea cookies or tea samples to the service desk folks because their customers would need a relaxing place to wait for the enormous car bill they were anxiously trying to not think about. I had fun walking around or looking at the Google map and thinking about my customer and where they may be. There was a dance studio up the street from my store, and moms would congregate at my shop while waiting for their children to finish practice. After me, they'd maybe drop into the nearby Italian deli and pick up dinner on their way home. Those were great outlets to partner with and display each other's marketing materials. By the end of my reign at the tea shop, 50 percent of my marketing strategy involved reaching customers who were already in our neighborhood— easy to reach and at essentially no cost. I still needed to reach new customers because we weren't in the class A real estate area of town (where foot traffic was given and rents were startup–prohibitive). But I was in a town where growth through development was prevalent, so I also spent some time researching public and private development plans (nearby construction will affect revenue), information on nearby businesses, and pertinent regulations and ordinances. Commercial real estate listings provide a lot of this information, including traffic counts, to help you scope the market as part of your research.

Building your marketing plan takes time, but how much relates to how far you want to go. I recommend one to five days of pure research, then bake into your timeline some market analysis, to convince people who just don't get it. My landlord was concerned about my marketing plan because in 2012, he didn't view social media and the vehicles I selected *Timeline Tip* as strategy. In his experience, traditional mailing lists needed to be leveraged and more money needed to be thrown at the marketing effort. Yet, he was the first to tell me (repeatedly) how impressed he was with my newsletters and my ability to speak to a demographic of ladies far beyond my years who got engaged with social media because the community invited them. He would forward my digital media to other tenants and suggest they follow suit, so their rent came in on time! Talk about validation.

Not sure if you should double down on LinkedIn or speakers' bureaus? Can't seem to settle on Facebook or Instagram as your primary vehicle to reach prospective customers? If drilling down on your marketing mix is overwhelming, know that you're not alone and the only way you can really know is to try. Hubspot is a great resource to talk you through what your blog should look like, or what your best bets for social media vehicles are. Recognize that what you start with in your plan doesn't have to be the vehicle that carries you to an initial public offering (IPO). It has to make sense for the first six to twelve months, and it must be your best educated guess. With my master's in business administration, I could comfortably apply statistics to marketing and calculate strategic approaches, but I had never learned *how* to market a business. Business school never will teach you how, because it's different for every business. Comfort yourself that you don't need an MBA to apply thought and calculations on what you expect a return to be on a marketing ad campaign or hopeful net impact of joining a referral group, for instance. Even free marketing tools cost money in terms of your time and if you elect to advertise through them, so build your plan around the vehicle where your audience is and try to stick to tools that are useful to you. When I first started out, some folks recommended Tumbler and Twuffer (Twitter-specific tweet scheduler), which for me were just other systems to dedicate time to, to broaden my reach. I used Hootsuite a lot because I could schedule across platforms and maximize the efficiency of my Marketing Mondays. Full disclosure on Hootsuite: If someone was looking at my Facebook page for how active I was or scrolling for content on Twitter, it was effective. But because Facebook changed its algorithms what felt like monthly, not many people saw my Hootsuite-scheduled posts after Facebook began allowing postdated posts, so I ended up considering whether even Hootsuite was worth my time. Unless it's the golden egg of social media (right now that's Instagram, but even that is getting bogged down with ads) it will run its course and it may or may not make sense for reaching your customer. If you believe spending money on a campaign is a good use of coveted startup funds, plan to commit for several months (run the campaign for weeks here and there, but don't abandon the tool until you've had a chance to evaluate it). Always evaluate after each campaign or at minimum every six months for ROI. If your followers are slowly growing and you're seeing some results, it's worth keeping, but then layer in another vehicle to see if there are other tools to really maximize your marketing efforts.

Another effective marketing reach was when local bloggers or customers added me to "best of" lists. The sites who offer these lists usually try to upsell you an ad when the list is published (it's a sales tactic for them usually). And it's surely a popularity contest (how many votes can you get?!) but it does get your name out to a much larger list of subscribers and there are, of course, bragging rights. If that's not feasible for your business, try Audiencebloom.com/resources as another good lead to increase your exposure. Some of these are hard to guarantee (winning "best of" awards), so I wouldn't put it in your primary marketing plan, but it is perhaps worth knowing the times of year they come out, so you can ask your followers to vote in subsequent quarters.

So much of your revenue scheme will come from sketching your marketing template and determining what makes the most sense for your company. What made the most sense for my company? Yelp was by far the most effective. So many people use Yelp to answer their questions ("reflexology near me," "best chai in Arlington, VA," etc.), and it plays into Google SEO relevance, since Yelp reviews tend to be some of the top results in Google searches. People found me, they fed it with pictures and reviews, and I benefited tremendously from this free service to businesses. I did eventually try out the Yelp ads (where you get placed on competitors' pages first), but I really didn't need it. Plus, it was expensive. I didn't see a tremendous increase in customers given the uniqueness of my business, but my sister was pleased with her ads for her yoga studio, because the market was much more competitive. Sticking to the free version won't work for every business, but Yelp gets the public to reach you. It also gives people a free platform to engage with you and empowers them to support your business and really stand behind their word, which is a powerful thing. Even private practitioners or consultants can have a Yelp page, and it helps validate the business, qualify the service, and, as mentioned, helps with SEO rankings because of the number of users. Where it makes sense for your business, it is worth setting up a Yelp page.

I want to note that there are plenty of online lists like Yelp to join (trade associations, TripAdvisor, Angie's List, Vegan Lovers, Local Makers, Things to Do . . . if there is an industry, there is a list or twenty around it). A lotta people make a lotta money by listing you! Many are free to register, but to really use it as a vehicle to intrigue customers, you'd need to elect for premium profiling. This could mean paying more to link your website, upload your menu, have more than one picture, etc. If it's a reputable list that your customer is bound to find you on, it may be worth it. But beyond the cost, being on every single list is a lot to manage. Anytime your hours change or your menu changes (if they won't link directly to your site's menu for free—some platforms offer this as a premium service), it becomes a lot of work to keep up with.

At the end of the day, your marketing should drive traffic to your site because there's invariably a call to action there, something that invites customers to schedule an appointment with you, buy from you, or sign up to hear more from you (so you stay relevant in their world). When I was in business, getting site traffic was nearly as important (at least to the marketing gods) as having a good brand and delivering a solid product. The way this was measured was through SEO. I spent a lot of time trying to understand keywords, how to use them, what aspects of each page needed more relevance, and how to better use social media and videos to increase that magic optimization number.

At the end of the day, your marketing should drive traffic to your site because there's invariably a call to action.

But you shouldn't throw all of your resources at SEO, especially if you have other ways to create loyal customers (by meeting them at craft fairs or coffee shops, for instance). This was true for my tea shop. I even tried to pay some SEO professionals to help put me on a path to SEO excellence, but most (at least the honest ones) wouldn't recommend their programs for my business because the value I delivered through the experience could do more for my reach than some inauthentic and only temporarily relevant algorithm. Similarly, more sage advice (at least at the time of writing) is to only try a social media marketing campaign if you really have something exciting to share (not your standard line). It's easy to overdo it and make people feel like you're just another company trying to reach them through the invasive means of the interwebs. Write a good blog and an engaging newsletter. Grow organically until you have something really exciting to talk about. Then when you're in a groove of what to promote and advertise, you can build your future marketing budget around releases or key partnerships.

All of these thoughts should be solidifying your marketing plan. Remember that you don't want to put every single idea down in the marketing plan, but to the extent that it reaches a certain customer or is in line with a plan to broaden your net, mention it. The rest of the ideas can always go into your strategic plan, introduced at the end of this planning chapter. The business plan should ultimately inform your strategic plan, so keep that in mind if your idea doesn't necessarily fit but you want to keep track of it until you have a better handle on budget and/or customer response. Bottom line, you want to start small, evolve fast, and get your customer to grow along with you.

In 2019, if you could only do three things for your digital marketing plan, it would be a website that houses thought leadership in its blog, bookmarking and sharing your content, and making some videos (no matter your trade). While it's a lot to think about, this is the fun planning, when you're not trying to plan *and* run a business, so enjoy it. Planning for financials might deflate your gorgeous balloon of purpose-filled visions, so really explore the possibilities through mar-

> *Bottom line, you want to start small, evolve fast, and get your customer to grow along with you.*

keting planning. Testing your ideas with some research to back them and time to see them play out will help you figure out which ideas are better than others (at least in your critical first year). From there, you can determine what can be fiddled with when the baby can sit up, freeing your hands a bit. So get inspired and aspire to do great things! Unless numbers are your thing, the next parts of the planning may withdraw from your "enthusiasm account," so for now, take in the excitement of ways you'll reach your customer. Unfortunately, only 2 percent of women-owned businesses hit the $2 million mark, so to make that number grow (if that is what your business is meant to be for you), believe in your marketing and believe in yourself, and you will make it happen when the time is right.

The above sections arguably define three P's of textbook marketing: product, placement, and promotion. The other piece of marketing is price, and this is the bridge between the marketing and financial planning sections of the business plan.

Document the ideas that come to you as you create the specifics of your marketing makeup. By going through this exercise, you should have concrete numbers to input into your financials, and as a result of fully working through the 4 P's, you may end up tweaking your financials a bit. If your ideal customers can't afford your entry point, perhaps you work more on volume, or you create a tier of offerings that meets your customer where they are and then a second tier once they're invested and can serve your business needs. That's the beautiful part of this process; you get to make your offerings make sense for you *and* your market. The basic approaches to price setting include

- ▶ value pricing (discount/market penetration)
- ▶ keystoning (markup from wholesale pricing)

- ▶ cost-plus (your cost plus a standard markup)
- ▶ psychological pricing (.99 instead of rounding up)
- ▶ bundle pricing (packaging things together)

The marketplace, how competitive the landscape, how disruptive you plan to be, your appetite for risk, and lots of other fit-for-business variables will come into deciding which pricing strategy makes the most sense.

Pro Tip

If you're planning to run monthly sales for whichever holidays are in play, price accordingly. But really think about those promotions because it's a lot of work for you, and customers begin to wait until your next promotion before buying. Beware of strategies that backfire.

How Do I Set My Price?

Product Business	Service Business
Whether cost-plus or market-based pricing, ensure every single cost is factored in.	Cost of salary, taxes, benefits and overhead plus roughly 30% (minimum) markup.
Research all the ways to price (dynamic pricing or discount pricing are also available, but complex to track for first time entrepreneurs).	Factor in risk, market, and enhanced values.
You can play around with product pricing strategies, but explore NOLO's Guide for great tips.	Don't forget to factor in vacation and personal time when determining your rate, setting a price that makes you feel whole.

Before leaving the topic of marketing, a very real part of it is the messaging, and often in business that can come in the form of a pitch deck. To draw an important clarification, an elevator pitch is the thirty-second speech you offer to an-y-one who will gift you that half a minute. You never know who is listening or who may have or know someone with deep pockets or valuable insights. The pitch deck, however, is a visual aid to the business plan and is most applicable for companies that require investors. If a pitch deck is in your future, be sure to check out appendix 2, which baby-steps you through a helpful deck. Even if you don't have plans for investors, why not have a look to think bigger and prepare you for greatness!

Step 2: Make the Numbers *Really* Work

The first step in building financials is to list out the costs to your plans. Take those revenue streams you dreamed up in the marketing plan and think about every single cost associated with them—packaging, shipping the packaging to you if it's a physical product, parking for client meetings, research and development if it's a service offering, and so on. After looking at your costs, organize them into fixed or variable costs. Usually there are costs related to having a physical site, web presence, or other startup or recurring costs. Then consider if there are sales or variable costs associated with transactions, like shipping to final destination or cost of goods sold.

Also, try to inform your projections with as much accurate vendor information as possible. Get written quotes and information locked in so you won't have to backtrack later when you're ready to act on a deal you negotiated. Speaking of negotiations, remember that *everything* can be negotiated (shipping, credit card rates, PayPal, utilities, and so on). For anything you'll use often or regularly, you can ask for better rates, and revisit them frequently. If you're only shipping five times a month, you may not have the bargaining position of someone whose business relies on the service, but it's worth meeting an account rep to learn if there are setup fees and what they can do to help you manage this cost. Even small savings could be the difference between red and black numbers each month.

Staffing levels should be broken out by role and budgeted as full time equivalents.

Use monthly periods to break up actual spending. Amortize quarterly expenses equally over a three-month period during projections.

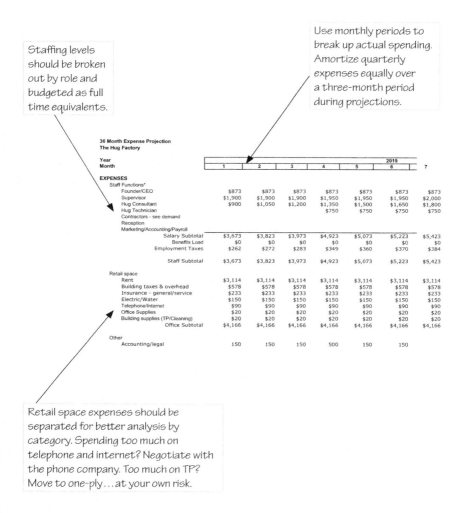

36 Month Expense Projection
The Hug Factory

						2019	
Month	**1**	**2**	**3**	**4**	**5**	**6**	**7**
EXPENSES							
Staff Functions*							
Founder/CEO	$873	$873	$873	$873	$873	$873	$873
Supervisor	$1,900	$1,900	$1,900	$1,950	$1,950	$1,950	$2,000
Hug Consultant	$900	$1,050	$1,200	$1,350	$1,500	$1,650	$1,800
Hug Technician				$750	$750	$750	$750
Contractors - see demand							
Reception							
Marketing/Accounting/Payroll							
Salary Subtotal	$3,673	$3,823	$3,973	$4,923	$5,073	$5,223	$5,423
Benefits Load	$0	$0	$0	$0	$0	$0	$0
Employment Taxes	$262	$272	$283	$349	$360	$370	$384
Staff Subtotal	$3,673	$3,823	$3,973	$4,923	$5,073	$5,223	$5,423
Retail space							
Rent	$3,114	$3,114	$3,114	$3,114	$3,114	$3,114	$3,114
Building taxes & overhead	$578	$578	$578	$578	$578	$578	$578
Insurance - general/service	$233	$233	$233	$233	$233	$233	$233
Electric/Water	$150	$150	$150	$150	$150	$150	$150
Telephone/Internet	$90	$90	$90	$90	$90	$90	$90
Office Supplies	$20	$20	$20	$20	$20	$20	$20
Building supplies (TP/Cleaning)	$20	$20	$20	$20	$20	$20	$20
Office Subtotal	$4,166	$4,166	$4,166	$4,166	$4,166	$4,166	$4,166
Other							
Accounting/legal	150	150	150	500	150	150	

Retail space expenses should be separated for better analysis by category. Spending too much on telephone and internet? Negotiate with the phone company. Too much on TP? Move to one-ply…at your own risk.

Every single business (unless cash only) will get to share their hard-earned profits with big credit card companies who make their money off of you getting paid, usually to the tune of 2–3 percent. The payment-processing industry has become more streamlined in the past few years, but if you're still working with a physical POS system, or if you have multiple ways to get paid (website, in person, Square, etc.), it's important to understand credit card/online merchant fees and adjust your price to account for these when building your projections. In other words, not only do these costs need to be smartly represented on your financials, your price needs to take these fees into account. More specifically, the company who deposits your funds into your account has their fee (usually about 2 percent), and sometimes Visa/Mastercard also have exchange fees. And sometimes there's a monthly fee, fees for returns, chargebacks, and more (in the fine print, of course). If you're doing a lot of volume, or if you're able to minimize fraud or chargebacks (like requiring a zip code or security combination in the transaction), you can sometimes get better rates. If your future vendor has a sales rep (even cloud-based POS systems do), it's definitely worth talking through your business with them to see if there is any flexibility on the rate or setup fees given the nuances of your business. And while this doesn't happen so much with current industry, sometimes there are term requirements associated with being your merchant service provider. These words of wisdom are to help you understand all the costs of your business, but also to suggest that you compare a few companies to understand that some come in the form of a higher flat rate, some come in the form of fees and per-transaction variables, but all are passing costs on to you.

The same goes for payroll processing and gift card fees. The base rate looks attractive, but if you feel like you're getting a steal, you should definitely sleep on it. Chances are, there could be exchange fees or other ways that would negatively affect your bottom line if not accounted for. You may still end up going with the vendor with the steal, but you'll have more peace knowing you've taken the time to truly understand what's behind the makeup and factored that into your planning.

Pricing. Now that you've laid out your costs, consider if you could get by with a competitive price in the beginning but, once you're working with clients and have less time to connect with your pipeline, charge more to cover a social media intern to keep your funnel fueled. Your price in the beginning should take into account your price in three years. Remember, your lean startup is intended to grow, and that costs money. Your price will need to cover it because you'll need your margins for lessons your business is here to teach you. Be prepared to increase price each year, or if that doesn't feel right, set a price that allows you to try on strategies when you're beyond the tight belt stage.

I had a lovely line item for the gift card revenue we'd be bringing in, and I'd even researched the attrition rate of how often they're redeemed (the odds of redemption after sixty days drops dramatically!) but failed to factor in the $30/month fee or the $1 per card requirement to have the cards be electronic. It was a necessary cost to have the reporting and ease of redemption for my customers, but a forgotten expense that went straight to my bottom line. Even taking time with the numbers, I still had forgotten fees. Having your business plan laid out in terms of revenue streams and associated fees will serve you when it's time to set up your budget accounts for QuickBooks, FreshBooks, or any other software you'll use. This fixed cost is the best money you'll spend (if it's sized right for your business: complex businesses need complex tools, and the reverse is true, too). Note that if your calculations suggest you can't afford tools like this but still can afford your business, you can start out with free tools like Mint. com, although I urge you to think bigger for the important tools like managing the growth of your company: it's an investment in your scalability. If you'll need to offer estimates that turn easily into invoices, or track hours related to billables, think bigger.

Taxes. Next, think about who is interested in a bite of your baby. Some sources recommend applying a blanket 30 percent for taxes when doing projections, although I did that initially and found myself revisiting the projections pretty quickly once I started having conversations with other business owners. I needed to estimate a lot more real estate tax than other areas, and the business license tax was a different rate based on what and how much I sold. While I thought I was being comprehensive by figuring out the various sales and meals tax rates, which were tied to revenue anyway, I failed to include the huge chunk of cash I needed to pay the county in tangibles tax (property tax for businesses) for the equipment I was using to conduct business. While these fees didn't break the bank, they certainly cut into margins in those early years.

When thinking about the tax implications of each of your revenue streams, it's best to check with your local jurisdiction or county website. This is the governing body that will ultimately be the first level of tax, and it issues your business license that allows you to legally collect revenue. Naturally, they have a wealth of information for anyone who is thinking about making (them) money through a business startup. Some counties have more requirements than others, but this resource should help you gauge the guidelines on licensing, determine how much is involved with each step, and piece together what is needed for your particular industry. Some sophisticated jurisdictions have BizLaunch or similarly named unit that helps you navigate the sea of permits and regulations, as well as general support for startups and nonprofits. If your county hasn't invested in programs to help businesses navigate, look at the Arlington County, Virginia, website. And if you're close enough, maybe you can attend their lectures and seminars on the aforementioned topics. When I quit my job entirely too early, I used the extra time to attend many of these seminars. While I regretted quitting so early when it took eighteen months to get to my opening launch (I may have mentioned that retail spaces can create unintentional delays), being able to attend the seminars was invaluable to my readiness. Plus, I met some really great contacts early on, both fellow business parents and influential bankers and county representatives who helped make the processes smoother. And the time wasn't entirely lost: In writing this book, I'm bringing many of those lessons to you!

In summary, many local jurisdictions can offer a complete list of what taxes would apply to you, and I encourage you to consult with a CPA who works with small businesses in your state and county who can advise you on all the taxes (it's usually a business license tax, tangible personal property tax, unemployment tax, employer income tax, sales/use/meals tax, even down to a litter or recycle tax). State taxes are often included on local jurisdiction summaries, but if not, make sure you visit your state's taxation page for taxes and regulations that apply to your business.

Planning for federal taxes will mostly depend on how you're structured. You'll want to decide this before you finalize your projections. Another thing to think about in your type of entity is *how* you'll be doing business. Initially, I had assumed I might be able to deduct the requests for charity donations that come because everyone assumes that businesses make money and therefore have money. Or that you need more customers and their cause will net you the customers you need from their "free" marketing opportunity. While it's true that lots of things are deductible (and it really does feel nice to be able to help your community), charitable contributions are not, *unless* you register yourself as a corporation. On the other hand, accountant fees, bank charges, bookkeeping software and fees, compensation/payroll, food samples to public, heating and utilities rent, overhead *are* all deductible, so maybe it comes out in the wash. Unless you plan to be heavily involved in the community and will be making these donations anyhow, I wouldn't necessarily change your status just for this deduction, but it's good to know before giving thousands of dollars in gift cards or products away in your first year. Plenty to consider as you settle on your legal structure. Don't stress, you can change it later, but for now, give it as much healthy thought as you can.

If you haven't decided yet, now's the time: how you'll organize your baby business.

Timeline Tip

Now that you've seen on paper that there is a viable business, take a moment to think black and white about the future (as best you can). If you don't have access to an accountant or lawyer to help you navigate the implications of selecting your business entity, be prepared to do some legwork. Most new parents go the LLC route, but so much depends on how your business will interact with your personal situation. Consider these helpful resources:

▶ sba.gov
▶ inc.com guides
▶ themoneyalert.com (http://themoneyalert.com/Corp -Entity-Table.html)
▶ NOLO's Guide to Business Taxes. This will help you repeatedly. It's also worth looking into considering what deductions you might be interested in claiming, which will affect what type of entity you might become.
▶ *475 Tax Deductions for Your Business and Self-Employed Individuals*, by Bernard Kamoroff (10th edition).

While doing your financial planning and looking at the levels of taxes, you may be tempted to go ahead and register yourself for the various taxation departments when you're already on the website. You can generally wait to register the tax aspects of your business, both state (sales/use or meals) and jurisdiction/county (meals—yes, sometimes at both levels—or business license), closer to when you'll be buying wholesale or closer to when you'll have your one location set. I went ahead and registered early for my sales tax, thinking my online store would generate revenue until the storefront was open, and used my home address when registering. When the retail space opened and I was myopically focused on making revenue to pay the rent and the wages, I forgot that I'd been reporting taxes from one address while it was registered to another. Luckily, the state was understanding and removed the late penalties for not filing with my home address until I got it cleared up. It was all the same EIN number, but they had no idea whether I was operating in one location or two. For all they knew, I could have been running the online portion of my business from home and the cafe portion from the storefront. If you do end up registering for your sales tax (if you will be selling products; not applicable for service providers), you will still need to file a zero return for any months you do not collect revenue in the beginning. It takes thirty seconds and avoids late fees, and on the upswing, even filing zero returns provides more times your business has been on record as filing taxes on time, if anyone ever looks into your business practices (hopefully not!). Besides, being in the habit of filing these taxes is a good rhythm to be in and one less thing to incorporate when orders are coming in and you're focused on customer service and quality delivery.

Planning to Protect Yourself

Don't forget about protecting your risk exposure. I knew I needed some basic coverage, but an insurance specialist looked at my business plan, pointing out various philanthropic goals like featuring local artists, and illustrated what would happen to their life's work hanging on my walls if there was a fire. In building your expected costs, speak with an insurance broker (or three) to assess how much cost your coverage will involve.

While entirely optional, other risk-minimizing efforts include securing a trademark or patent if your idea is unique. It may be more important if your business is technology-based and will be part of your valuation upon exit. You first need to ask yourself what you are protecting. There is a lot of value in getting a patent, especially to prospective investors, if you know you're going to have to raise some capital before you can birth your baby. Eventually the $250 per use investment could be worth something, but in the beginning, it is a legal hoop to work through. The fees start piling up when you use an attorney to help you file (it's not the most intuitive process) and six months after they accept the filing, you'll have to pay another $200 to verify its use. An attorney isn't necessary per se, but they do help translating the scary forms and are of value when it comes time to refile several years down the road after you've forgotten all about your little trademark.

Pro Tip

Once you're on file with the US Patent and Trademark Office, your information will be available to everyone (including other countries) who will tell you that you need to pay them to protect your name under whatever list or country they're representing. *None of that is legit.*

As for when to file for your employer tax requirements and receive your federal Employer Identification Number (form SS-4) from the IRS, you'll need this shortly after registering your business and before you apply for state tax status (for wholesale, for instance). This is required for all businesses, even if you don't have any employees other than yourself, and will be a number that the banks require before you can set up a bank account or request a loan. If you'll have employees, you'll need to also register with your state's employment commission. General navigation advice on this can be found in appendix 4.

If you've made it this far in your plans, you're doing great and demonstrating that you can dig in and focus on the end result, which is a virtue that marks a successful entrepreneur. The details can at times be overwhelming. Take a deep breath and maybe a day off from all the thinking and then return to your plan with fresh eyes. I like to reconnect with my softer side when I've had to spend time in "yang" space of numbers and planning. Connecting with a more feminine side is a tip I learned from another mom business owner. Anytime she had to do her invoicing and payroll, she always burned a candle to soften the experience. Naturally more yin myself, if I need to engage with harder, detailed planning, I use ambient music and some essential oils to relax (lavender and frankincense) and remind myself that it's an honor to do this for my business.

Step 3: Get Some Feedback

After working your finance and marketing plans, pay a visit to the Small Business Administration website. They have an abundance of information, checklists, and best of all a host of volunteers (through their SCORE and Small Business Development Center programs throughout the country) who meet with expecting business parents and help them with their budgeting, marketing research and plans, and legal advice. This is a tremendous resource and can help you think in terms you might not have or help poke holes in or positively reinforce your ideas. Just remember it's free, and you can't expect the same level of detail/knowledge from a volunteer who spends one hour on your business as you could if hiring a professional or coach. But free is freedom to choose to spend your money other ways, so it's still a really good resource. If not in person, their website still offers plenty of general information and also advice on laws and regulations. It even offers podcasts, forms, fact sheets, and more.

Have all of your numbers (the first two to three years) ready for feedback. Anticipate any growth costs (new product designs, new reaches, additional employees) or, as hard as it is to imagine when you haven't even purchased anything, the likelihood for breakage or slippage. Equipment, even computers, printers, or props will need replacing in the first few years, especially if you're choosing cheaper options to begin with because you're bootstrapping. Thinking about those costs now will give you peace later. The decision will still very likely be economical, but knowing what you're buying now can impact your year 2 and year 3 costs. And the skillful eyes of SCORE counselors can help validate or dismiss areas of your predictions.

If all of this seems daunting, it's supposed to be. Anything worth having is worth working for, so love this process as much as you can. You won't regret being over prepared for this portion of your first business journey and I feel certain that by spending time thinking about your industry in different ways, new ideas will emerge. If you find yourself more anxious or fearful after doing this legwork, that's a good thing, too. These feelings are surfacing for a reason. Tuning into them and deciding what to do with them is the best thing you can do at this point, before you spend more money and time on this life-changing endeavor. Take another pregnant pause and figure out what the fear is telling you. If informed by unattractive financials, fear could reveal a need for an additional revenue stream, or possibly that this is the end of the road. Alternatively, it could be a healthy vehicle to navigating the road ahead with confidence that there's something to gain. With any of these results, you're getting wonderful information.

Expect Financing (Most Likely)

First, consider burning a candle or putting on a pot of tea before working through this section. Next, consider this story: Once upon a time, a dream needed $50,000 to carry operations until revenue began flowing. The financials suggested there was a chance the baby could be born without investment, but the mama-to-be couldn't predict the future so decided to embark on the painful process of applying for a loan to buy some peace of mind.

If you see outside funding in your future, the financial work continues. The basic projections already outlined need to answer the questions of how much you'll make and how much you can reinvest in the business after taking your cut (your margin). If you're going for financing, you'll need to be more detailed, often to the tune of multiple reports such as cash flow/income statements, contribution margin, fixed operating expenses, taxes, and net profit, as these are the main reporting elements to predicting success. These five data points (plus balance sheets if your business is a little further along) are what many financiers will want to know you've thought about.

Reports You'll Need for Financing

- ▶ Cash-flow/income statements
- ▶ Contribution margin
- ▶ Fixed operating expenses
- ▶ Taxes
- ▶ Net profit
- ▶ Balance sheets (maybe)

Why do they matter? You can easily say how you'll make money, but to make money you have to spend money, and it's important to think about where that money will come from, in a variety of scenarios such as worst case, best case, and average of the two. Cash flow can and does ruin businesses. Having some honest conversations with yourself will pay proverbial dividends in your future. Some people refuse to put any money into their business venture, and that may mean really getting creative. A good tip is to weave the business into personal planning (family vacations, kids going to private school, etc.). This is especially helpful if you're an LLC (where you include business gains or losses in your personal tax filing), and although you're not putting up your savings to fund your dream, you're still putting up your time and that may mean more childcare and less time working a job that used to fund vacations or nights out. Seeing exactly how the business integrates into your life on paper can drive how you work later. In other words, if you don't need to repay yourself but you do need to repay a loan, your behavior may be different. Try to keep this in mind when figuring out if your business requires some form of financing beyond bootstrapping.

Typically, startups don't have a lot of equity, so most of their financing is in the form of debt financing (as opposed to equity financing). Whichever type of lending, the goal should be to not leverage yourself beyond the point of healthy operations, meaning the interest or cost to service the equity won't be so high that cash flow is impeded. If you'll be financing your business through equity and shares, it's best to get an accountant and lawyer to walk you through this and get your agreements set up accordingly. If financing through debt, having the right debt to equity ratio is something banks will consider (and you should research further) but still doesn't guarantee you'll get a business loan. There are many factors used to evaluate a business, such as net worth (the equity in a business, often a combination of retained earnings and owner's equity), confirmed sales or letters of intent, historical sales (impossible for a startup), and how much the guarantor can collateralize. I learned a great deal about the financing process from a seminar hosted by my local BizLaunch team (through my county's economic development programs) and a bank that was hoping to get a few new customers out of the gig. In reality, most startups' options are very limited, and getting creative is the name of the financing game. Pure startups (younger than two or three years, by most standards) are generally not attractive to banks: many businesses are lucky to make it past two years, which is when a lot of loan terms are beginning to call due. I do believe, though, that if this baby is growing inside you, you'll find a way. It might have to be a partial launch if the traditional financing doesn't work out, but don't let banks intimidate you too much. Take their information and decide what you can do with it.

Heard good things from the government about "just" getting an SBA loan? The truth is that even with an awesome ratio (read, all of your savings and no debt and a very low–cost startup model), most startups won't qualify for what the SBA considers "small business" loans. The requirements for said loans are quite high and the interest rate is large and probably not something a bootstrapping entrepreneur should wisely accept. And many SBA loans are not approved. (In my case, I hadn't shown the established income necessary for several

SBA-approved banks to work with me.) Even if you do get an SBA loan, take a personal loan or leverage the equity in your home like I did. All financiers will want collateral, so it's not only your savings you're putting on the line. If you're borrowing $100,000, you'll still need $80,000 to collateralize the loan, so hopefully you have that much in equity. Or a really expensive car, but if that's the case, you should sell the car because you'll pay at least market rate *plus* 4–5 percent (for a total of 8 percent or more for using the government's SBA programs). Assuming they accept you and your business plan. Sadly, they are primarily set up to fund existing businesses that have two to three years' worth of steady financials. Your best bet is to find another source that won't cost you significant fees and interest, and that requires a payback in five or more years.

And one more mama-to-mama warning: beyond reserving cash for your daily operations, recall that the fastest way to choke your business is to grow. In other words, if significant growth is planned in the first three years (of course it is), beware of overleveraging yourself; you can tie up all your money in returning your cash to the bank or investors instead of investing in important systems or growth enhancements. This happened with Starbucks in its infancy, too, when they purchased Peete's Coffee to help expand in the 1980s. Being so overleveraged, the company would quickly learn that its traditional growth and innovation were, at that moment, no longer within financial reach.

Modern entrepreneurs have found ways around this problem via crowdfunding, but there are still a lot of questions and limitation around this, so explore if it's right for your business. For instance, certain platforms require you to meet the minimum goal before you'll be paid. Others charge high fees and limit the types of businesses that can participate, and some have come under scrutiny for what the "investment" purports to the donor; some contributors thought they were buying a piece of the company when they decided to fund a particular business. While crowdfunding is not a bad idea if you have a really unique concept and a clear illustration of how the money will be used, do the research first and know the limitations. Some colleagues of mine turned their coffee-roasting business into a coffee storefront and have been doing great in the DC metro area. They used EquityEats to help fund their startup. Similar companies have come on line as well to make the difference in what you can afford through the help of consumer investors (with a set, usually affordable entry fee in exchange for lifetime goods/services). There are many other crowd-sourcing ways to try to fund your business, but all of them must tie back to the projections.

Real-Life Example

I had a colleague from business school who started an online suit company for women. At the time there was nothing like it for women, and to help their operations, $100, which was the cost of materials and fabrication, could secure your first suit, make you a believer, test their supply chain, and ultimately get their company off the ground. Except once they had met their crowdsourcing goal, their supplier relationship changed and suddenly their new option cost them far more than $100 to build and they were back at square one with quality control. They would not have enough to fund the suit orders, and they ended up offering to repay everyone their initial investment because they found themselves more than a year out from newly defined operations and multiple financing hurdles away from being able to truly launch the company. On the bright side, they needed to learn that lesson, and thankfully they had "early believers" to figure that out with, instead of high-expectation customers.

By now it probably seems there isn't a fast and easy way to get financed, and that's because unless you have a wealthy benefactor, not many entities are dying to throw money at unlikely odds (startups are rarely a fast ROI). Don't let financing burst your baby bubble entirely.

There are opportunities for alternative financing, but they can come at the expense of your potentially already fragile relationships. Most everyone advises to look to the three F's: Friends, Family, and other Fools. They're called fools because it's probably not a "loan" unless you're in the fortunate 10 percent of businesses that succeed wildly. These people are the easiest source of funds. The term "bootstrapping" is also considered a means of finance that includes the personal use of savings, credit cards, second mortgages, customer advances, and vendor credit (ok, that last one is perhaps not that common, but maybe you're really lucky and have a good relationship with your sales rep). Also available but trickier are venture capitalists, but not without promising your firstborn and a lot of control of your business and usually only if you're seeking $5 million or more; angel investors (you might be in the lucky 5–10 percent of solopreneurs to get funded this way), or government programs (female/minority benefits if your business is in government contracting). A quick note: these government programs are more often designed for small businesses to find ways to earn contracts, and not as often cash grants left on the table, at least in my experience (nonprofits excluded). If your plan is solid and your concept compelling, you may be considered by an incubator or accelerator who can connect you to partners willing to help fund some of your startup costs, which is a funding source gaining popularity in larger cities in America. Some funding deals have been made with local development authorities, or through bartering or peer-lending groups, or in most cases, by partnering or becoming a joint venture with an existing company. Some jurisdictions also have incentives, whether it be in partnership with states or developers to attract certain types of business, but they are usually tied to performance, so you'd need to report back regularly as you would to investors. Once again, it's an option to explore but not without extensive research and a grain of skepticism. I ultimately ended up using a business credit card and the equity in our home, and while that was a huge savings (3 percent loan), it came at a significant cost to the relationship with my husband, who wanted that equity back . . . fast.

Business Credit Card

It's important, so go ahead and set one up if you can before buying a lot of things with your personal card. Even if you'll track the expenses separately, having a small balance card linked to your Employer Identification Number (EIN) will help your business build credit. If it is only costing you a few thousand dollars to get started and you could technically pull that from savings, you should still consider opening a credit card. You can pay off the balance if you have the means, but by doing so you earned your business a name for itself in credit agencies if you want to try for a business loan in the future.

Plenty. Common advice says to have cash or credit available to finance your startup costs plus six months' worth of operations (monthly fees, payroll, rent, etc.). Plenty of sources estimate you'll need three times that much, depending on how much exposure you have, meaning expensive equipment/up-front costs or hefty payroll, so buffering this number is wise. Most of those costs assume you're coming from a realistic position and that nothing breaks in your first year. This mama urges you to tuck away a little extra still, just to cover first-timer's decisions, because that year two wisdom is costly and your first year will not be perfect.

If you do find yourself in a pickle in that you didn't set aside or borrow enough, there are now sources like OnDeck or Kabbage.com that can lend you up to $50,000 on the spot for payroll, inventory, or whatever you need. These do come with high interest rates, but can be a safety net if needed. You can potentially get by with less in reserves if you plan to stay on part-time with your day job or do a moonlighting gig to help fund operations until your baby can feed itself. While the business will likely feel the trade-off, most bankers want to see that a borrower is still generating some income. In my case, I financed with pure hustle, reinvesting revenue in the company in the early days to tackle the loan quickly. Not knowing what to expect, I didn't want to take a paycheck (and be taxed on income) if I could hold tight till end of quarter to see how we did. Note that an investor prefers an owner to focus completely on the business. This is at odds with the security a side hustle brings, but in my experience, it seemed a little more valuable since loan payments come due quickly and the investor's portfolio is counting on that sweet interest. I had been offered an easy way to moonlight with my old company shortly after opening my business, and I had set up the storefront such that I was only a behind-the-scenes owner while I figured out how to eventually scale the business. This helped me tremendously in the first year because while we were doing well, exceeding projections and covering our operational costs, things broke and purchases I hadn't anticipated occurred—like sound dampeners for the acoustics, more towels and slippers for the foot sanctuary, backup storage for security cameras . . . it goes on. Moonlighting part-time didn't necessarily pay for these but did buy me sanity. The value of this approach also became apparent during the first summer. I had gotten pretty comfortable with the early results and was flatfooted when summer rolled around and our revenue dropped by more than 50 percent. Having a side hustle allowed me to cover the interest on the business loan when I was too fearful of spending due to low-income months. I wouldn't recommend reinvesting excess dividends in the business in the early days unless the possibility of a side hustle exists to keep you fed. If you didn't see this lesson coming, feed yourself first . . . and make sure you're planning for those food expenses, too.

If you're thinking of seeking investors, prepare to get intimate with whoever is lending you their cash. Like bringing on a partner, the exposure you will share will be much greater than if dealing with banks or some of the other financial options explored here. As illustrated in *Angel Investing: Matching Start-Up Funds with Start-Up Com-*

panies, by Mark Van Osnabrugge and Robert J. Robinson, you need to openly address risks and problems with your business and how they can best be overcome. He also says to try not to let fundraising adversely affect ongoing business operations. This means being smart about whom you seek funding from. If you're showing your plan to everyone, you're wasting your time. Be specific about your ideal investors. They also offer that angels are looking for opportunities to add their own skills/creativity to trustworthy entrepreneurs with a firm in a niche market. If you've got those attributes plus healthy financial projections, you might just get the investor you've dreamed of. Conversely, venture capitalists (VCs) look for experienced and well-balanced management teams and a developed firm, which is rarely a startup. So if you're seeking the level of funding VCs are capable of, you're probably in a proven niche market with nearly unlimited growth potential . . . and seriously crushing it as a mama-to-be!

Financing doesn't need to be an added stress. It's all about what you want, which doesn't have to be overwhelming.If you're content with your lifestyle business that has a solid financial model, you'll feel great having thought through your business and become even more convinced of your path. If you're invigorated, congratulations; this big milestone is where a lot of embryo businesses lose their way. If you can't find a way to finance your dream, try again in a few months. Plenty of lenders need different portfolios, and you can consider modifications to your grand plans, like maybe taking on a partner who can align with the mission and offer oversight while you go sell or perhaps bring a financial investment.

Indeed, there is a lot to digest. The realization that you can make money doing this thing you love is fun, even if the process of planning

---

Financing doesn't need to be an added stress. It's all about what you want, which doesn't have to be overwhelming.

---

isn't. Think of this as that awful calculator you can plug in to see how much having a baby will cost you in the first year: $28,000 for gear, care, food, and diapers? No way! Yet it's true and you somehow figure it out. Before you're totally done with all this thinking and getting comfortable with the uncomfortable aspects of your business, read *Why Companies Fail*, by Mark Ingebretsen, and look back at your plan to ensure you're not positioning yourself for some of the signs of potential demise, which include but aren't limited to (do your research or hire a coach if you can afford it) growing too fast, ignoring shifts, innovating too much, failed synergies, and greed or arrogance. This is where the strategic plan (a mirror of your business plan, but more detailed) comes into play. Even if you're totally set up for success on paper (the business plan), there's more. Layering in the diverse and widespread demands of being a business owner, and thinking about *how you're thinking* is important. And preparing yourself for sustainability is the missing piece to Ingebretsen's thesis. Refer back to the section on mental sustainability for a moment, then proceed to thinking about the nuances of your business.

As you begin to wrap up the primary nuts and bolts of your plan, remember that it should demonstrate that you've thought about your reality, calculated risks, and conducted cost/benefit analysis that this baby is still worth the making. It's important to identify risks in the business plan that investors may be considering, and also think about vulnerabilities in and threats for your strategic plan that dictates how you do business.

Expect Strategy

The strategic plan is what you hold yourself to and goes into a little more detail about the risks you need to prepare for. It mirrors the business plan in the marketing and priorities for revenue generation but goes much deeper into the *how* of business birthing and nurturing. This is especially important if you elect for the one-to-two-page business sketch. Basics that this addendum plan holds are potential ideas/

things that didn't make it into the marketing and finances for the first three years. This plan should also have the view of your future "'C suite" and what roles they would play if your company scaled beyond imagination (or even a healthy scale that you might not have anticipated in the first few years). If that's hard to imagine, picture a corporate company that serves the same market on a broader scale. What is the chief operation officer thinking about? Do you have a technology officer? It may seem silly to think so big if your company is positioned to be a one-woman shop into perpetuity, but if nothing else, this brainstorming exercise can help you think about some dynamics of your company that will eventually surface, so you might as well apply some mindfulness now. These are some things you can explore in your strategic plan:

▶ *Logistics (how/operations):* supply chain and careful planning of how you'll maximize your time or minimize your costs, employee manual plans, how-to's documented should someone need to step in and run your business (if you get pregnant in the actual sense, for instance). This is a huge part of my consulting business: business moms and dads haven't taken the time to document, and when they're suddenly in a pickle, it takes a really seasoned businessperson to assemble the pieces when they step in. Operations can so quickly be a drag to your business. Suddenly 80 percent of your energy goes to 20 percent of your revenue, which should be the other way round. Even if you don't have a solution for everything, you can at least start a list of things you do and would eventually outsource as part of your operations planning.

▶ *Team characteristics (who/talent/recruitment):* who you are/your capabilities and what complementary team characteristics look like, even how meetings can be conducted to align with your mission.

▶ *Risk exposure not spelled out in business plan:* avoiding employee theft, for example. Trademarks or having proprietary education materials online and steps to protect should be part of the overall business plan.

▶ *Technology (beyond if your printer breaks):* how much you will rely on technology. If you're not already tech savvy, it might be worth thinking through. Bootstrappers can't possibly have enterprise systems that connect all of the dots and ways we interface with technology, so the strategic plan is where you can start to build out what future investment in technology could look like. To illustrate this, I didn't bother researching internet bandwidth for what my POS and music systems were going to cost me. I had a technology consultant help me navigate this in a barter-for-tea arrangement. Technology is impossible to avoid, and there are plenty of how-to's on boosting your business using technology—creating a technology plan to improve cash flow, for instance. My MBA buddy was a product designer/project manager. She looked at my requirements, asked me questions I hadn't thought to ask myself about what my needs truly were (both from end user and back end capabilities), and drilled down on POS and online shopping carts that solved my needs and even matched my online imagery for a consistent user experience. I didn't even know what that was. We ultimately decided to go with a new company for the POS system because of its user simplicity and low entry cost. However, every time the company tried something new on their end, it created all kinds of learning curves and inconsistencies in our reporting. And each time we called for help, we got differing opinions because they were so new and they too were solving problems, live. Fortunately, their customer service was great and it all worked out. We felt in good company, both being startups and helping each other, but in the moment with frustrated customers, sometimes it wasn't so pleasant. In other tech bloopers, we wanted the phone not to ring in our shop because of the disruption to our ambiance. We wanted them to go to the website or leave a message and we'd call them back. The truth is, we were too busy to call them back right away and usually by the time we could call them to confirm that yes, we were open, they had found another place to meet their friend. So we set up the phone package as if we didn't need all the bells/whistles or the bandwidth and changed the script pretty early on when we realized most of our customers valued transacting over the phone rather than poking around the website (all part of learning our demographic). Bottom line, plan for flexibility as you learn, and keep technology in the front of mind as it relates to budget and ways it can enhance your business in the future.

▶ *Additional marketing (for those things that fell to the bottom of your list or are better investments once you hit the three-year milestone):* another place to keep track of what you want to do in the future as well as what you intend to do to check in on your marketing scheme. Year end is a great time to do this. You can plan to assess your ROIs via the various channels, reevaluate your marketing stack (the artifacts and brochures that tell your story), decide what worked well and what should be continued next year, and stand back from your metrics to not just measure, but manage what they're revealing. Year end is good since it's hard to pause frequently to evaluate helpful data points when in the thick of running a business.

▶ *Exit strategy:* exploring what the end goal is and if it's not achieved, what pivots might look like along the way. Building an exit strategy at the same time as building the business plan was ingrained in my head by my entrepreneurship professors. When you're in your first year, that horizon looks pretty fuzzy and may even change a bit. This is okay. I'm told that being open to possibilities is the mark of a good entrepreneur. But you need a guideline or framework. And when you do make it past the first two years, you should be able to revisit your goals and know that you're on your way even if the excitement has started to dwindle and you're wondering if you'll ever again be able to take a real vacation for more than two days. Even if the plan slides on the projections, at least it's there, and you'll stay more focused and feel a little lighter knowing there could be an exit, if desired.

The contents of a strategic plan may not be what a stakeholder looks, for but it is something you should consider as a guiding document. Don't think your business is so different that you don't need to have thoughts like sophisticated businesses. Study up on a few; maybe look at Apple's organization chart and think about how yours could learn from it. The strategic plan is a living document and doesn't need to be complete in order to move from planning into doing. Ninety percent of the strategic plan to this point can be dropped into a project management tool like Asana and organized for priorities from there. Remember, all this strategic planning speaks to feasibility and can help you determine where to focus and which areas make it into the monthly goals list when it's time to execute. It doesn't necessarily have to occupy space if it's part of the future plan. For me, the highest and best use of my time was marketing. This was apparent after I laid out all the educational topics, the alternative health, and offerings we could cover; and since I had a lot of this knowledge, I needed to get it into blogs/newsletters, etc., to help strengthen the brand. I left ordering and procurement to the team via checklists I helped create using the strategic plan, and I moved on. If nothing else, this appreciation helped me learn that I needed to delegate if I was going to get to any of the work that would keep us all employed. Even if you're a one-woman consulting shop, the strategic plan can help you prioritize your time and reflections, and can create guideposts for what aspects of your business could be given to an eventual assistant or intern.

	$ $ $	(desk worker)	(graph)	(people)
Desired outcome	Increase revenue 18% in FY20, 33% in FY 21.	Reduce overhead spending while maintaining A+ operations.	Expand presence in key markets and territories.	Contribute to the world as a corporate citizen in dollars and service hours.
FY19 strategies	Establish presence through launch in community business groups, conventions, and seminars, + traditional marketing efforts.	Encourage employees to bring their own device to save on hardware and telecom costs. Travel and convention/ seminar costs limited to senior officials.	Study case studies and market analysis to find underserved areas who fit our customer profile. Begin marketing program in Q3.	Instill quarterly community service dates for staff, as well as annual giving campaign outside of holiday season. Partner with local hospital for pro bono services.
FY20 strategies	Network beyond consumer level to launch new product lines, such as corporate consulting and teaming events.	Move to a remote workforce for experienced employees to reduce need for real estate costs. Savings target is 6% from previous year.	Aggressively build up marketing in Q1, with soft launch in late Q2. Fully expand in four key markets by start of Q4.	Continue to leverage quarterly community service dates with annual giving campaigns to connect with board members of partner hospitals.
FY21 strategies	Deliver and execute higher priced service offerings while expanding individual consumer services into new markets.	Negotiate terms for insurance, telecom, auto leases, and real estate. Savings target is 12% reduction from previous year.	Continue adding contiguous areas near five key markets while starting to identify next four areas to expand by Q2.	Strategically use relationships with board member partners to offer higher priced service offerings in existing and emerging markets.

Just as in life, best-laid plans are hard to keep, so use your plan as a guideline. Try to stick to your intended goals, but don't get too discouraged when things get sidetracked. It will happen, and you'll be a more malleable and robust business parent as a result of the lessons in flexibility that present themselves. The add-on message here is to pace yourself; there are so many elements to becoming a functioning business. This process helps you evaluate how fast and how fully you enter the market. Be it big splash or tiptoeing in, the answers will be clear for having thoroughly approached the planning process.

If you need to feel centered at this point, do some seated poses where you twist (cleanse) your spine and encourage fresh blood to pulse throughout the body. If you still need to relax further, let go and lie on the ground with your legs up a wall.

Nerves. This critical point can leave you feeling so ready or . . . so ready to walk away. If you truly feel like the signs are to quit, give it a few days, call your future board (members you may have met networking), and get their perspective. All this evaluation is healthy and almost a rite of passage for the introspection you've been doing. If your preparations are going strong despite the fears you've unearthed, this too is a big milestone considering all the energy and resources you've invested. If you're wary but still committed, try this: *Imagine what's possible after the risks are calculated, and create a sacred place for all of the tiresome and the lovely. If you still truly believe in your plan, be the invitation it needs to come alive.* This alignment with a bigger purpose or broader narrative—one that is not made small by irrational or uncon-

Create a sacred place for all of the tiresome and the lovely.

trollable fears—is what it takes to create a healthy environment for your baby to thrive. The book *Sacred Commerce* talks about how the point of suffering is often the point where life is asking you to let go of something that no longer serves you and oneness. I serendipitously read this after I had put together my business plan and felt the pull to carry this concept to term but was allowing some doubt to cloud my clarity. The book invited me to embrace the areas I was uncertain about and view them as an opportunity. The book also invited me to accept the beautiful parts as the abundance they are ready to share with the world. I held the space while the shadows of fear moved through. I realized this baby business was not just a great idea from an opportunity or first-mover perspective but also because it was love asking to be given space to help others in the busy area we live in. This realization invited the possibilities. A memory of my late great-grand-mother Agnes who taught me to appreciate tea and herbs was one of them. She passed away more than fifteen years prior so wasn't front of mind when I was working through the plans. Yet I realized in that sacred space that she also had soaked her feet in Epsom salt; this was a unique concept matched to the tea house concept purely through a need to fill the margins in an additional way to connect to healthy relaxation. That's when the third leg of my *why* made sense and the permission (push) to move presented itself. Yes, the need was there and yes, tea and alternative health had to be reintroduced, but a rever-berating yes echoed in my family calling, asking me to draw on my heritage and bring this child to life.

If striving for perfection and fear of failure are still in the way but the numbers make sense, know that the plan and the baby will con-stantly grow. You're doing this to really feel the rewards of hard work not shared with a corporation or overhead, and to align with your purpose. So aim big. Go for it. Be brave and tenacious but self-aware enough to check yourself. This is a fundamental skill that entrepreneurs possess. You'll soon get comfortable with dreaming, sketching, evaluating, and then promptly executing, or else you will naturally select yourself out of business ownership. Detailed planning is the first of many ways your trust in yourself will strengthen.

So what's next after all that grueling evaluation? Look at your reality and think about the transition from your current job (or wherever you are now) to birthing your own baby company. All of that evaluation is largely for information gathering as a means to your dreams. If the plan is in place but the finances aren't, love it for the exercise in timing it revealed. You have options, even if the decision is not now.

The business plan process should take a week to fully flesh out: research, getting quiet with self, assembling team (mentally), revising variables or inputs after consideration. I completed my plans while I was scrutinizing business plans when working on my MBA. If you're not in the habit of studying business plans, I'd apply the 3x multiplier (introduced in Undeniable Business Skill #5) so you have time to get intimate with industry and competition as well. *Timeline Tip*

Expecting: Planning and Readiness

Thorough planning can spare your sanity down the road. Take it slow, get comfortable. Truly evaluate the balance between bootstrap and brand strength. The framing company Framebridge wasn't lean but had to be perfect. No stepwise iterations like some companies can offer. Of course you want it to be perfect, but if it's at the expense of other operations, consider if your company can start smaller (while the business plan process serves you continuously).

Even though this section is very detailed, to help you think through the nuances of good plans, keep your plan concise, be clear in key assumptions, leave out technical jargon.

Make value add be your marketing goal, rather than statistics or reach (while important, they can't replace building loyal followers through humble efforts to know the customer). Remember: start small, evolve fast, get your customers to grow along with you.

Planning is pretty simple. Four questions in marketing, five thoughts in finance, and one general catchall to address other vulnerabilities or longer-term plans in the strategic plan. To recap, those were:

▶   Who is your customer (and buying patterns)?
▶   What is your market (and competitors)?
▶   How will you market in light of #1 and #2?
▶   How will you make money, in light of #1, 2 and 3 (and when will you break even/what margin will be available to fund growth)?

and

▶   Pricing is a moving target: give it your best calculus and reevaluate in year two using your strategic plan.
▶   Financing means creatively solving for cash flow. Think of it that simply.
▶   There is no shame in lean. Plan to start small. Lean startup will help your learning curve and your own expectations. Every other entrepreneur has done it this way, whether they admit it or not. Their financial outlook was scary, defended, and bolstered at some point, I assure you.
▶   The more you think now, the less headache you'll have later.
▶   Honesty is your friend.

Do not quit your day job until your plans are solidified. Get to the point where the job is standing in the way of launching the business. There's plenty that could be done while moonlighting, particularly

▶ creating a website, marketing materials (ready for networking), terms and conditions
▶ researching and building systems (CRM, project management)
▶ developing employee paperwork, contracts, training manuals, process and procedures
▶ completing vendor paperwork
▶ attending trade shows: get inspired and get contacts; make sure you know you're not missing something but don't get overwhelmed; they've been in motion longer
▶ finding a female networking group that fits you (social reinforcement, accountability, problem solving, etc.)
▶ taking a sales course
▶ incorporating "attracting good things" exercises
▶ practicing saying yes only when it fills up your buckets
▶ creating product; filling online orders
▶ following industry trends/commenting/being relevant
▶ negotiating lease; lawyer on deck
▶ getting familiar with site plans, revisiting ramp, outdoor seating
▶ loading inventory into systems
▶ considering freshening up website pictures or planning posts for when you're busy after launch
▶ writing newsletters or media vehicles to stay in touch while launch is looming

☐ Your Readiness Journal

$\mathcal{S}$ketching from this section should be into the various types of plans. To save time, I would go ahead and create the plans within an electronic medium after you've done your initial whiteboarding of who your customer is and how your solution meets her tendencies and buying patterns. From there, it's really a best use of time to go straight to the spreadsheets to test your pricing and cost variables.

_____

_____

_____

_____

_____

_____

_____

_____

Plan to spend several days on the research and plugging and playing with numbers. Then set it down and try not to think about it for at least a day. Come back fresh and see what new information comes to you.

Part II

Pressure, Preparation, and Preoccupation

4

Going Public: The Announcement and the Arduous Work

Expect Pressure

I have to be honest, I made my baby business news public way sooner than I am telling you to do. I was in a funk with my day job, not because it wasn't rewarding but because I was ready for a change. In a big way. It was grueling, although I liked the people with whom I worked. There was available progression, yet I was not inspired. So while I didn't tell many people while the plan was in process, I wish I had synchronized my announcement with a few more concrete steps toward launch. Because I didn't, in short order after vocalizing my plans I had the pleasure of juggling those steps with the rush of responsibility, the molting of my old skin, and the investment I had to make in myself to put my money where my mouth was. With the first "I'm opening a relaxation business" assertion, my mind wouldn't let me work less hard, nor did my heart want to. It meant I would feel vulnerable in the unknown of what I was supposed to be doing or how I was supposed to be behaving. It meant I had to embrace the new pressure to prove I can do all the things. Eyes were on me, and inquiries about my experience were directed toward me. I got used to the follow-up question after my pitch, "Now, have you ever done this before?" from strangers and certainly from bankers and brokers. I had a lot to prove to everyone. The moment I first heard (the first of several times), "What business do you have in business?" was the moment the work actually began. Their skepticism motivated me to prove them wrong and refine my view of what a businessperson can look like. *Isn't starting a business hard enough without having to also think about how you're being judged?* I wasn't looking to match society's notion of what a successful business persona was, but I *was* looking to understand it and become a more evolved me that shows up *smelling* like business. *Three prior startup experiences? No, only tenacious me chasing my unique and courageous dream, since, you know, there's a first time for everything.* I was poised as an HR professional before, but being collected as an entrepreneur would help avoid those ridiculous questions from brazen people and get to the heart of the exchange. Still, I loved them for saying what others may have been thinking and for demonstrating to me that I needed to get serious about the ways I represented my dream. I began paying close attention to what other entrepreneurs talked about, how comfortable they appeared in their own skin, and I channeled their confidence and relaxed interest when engaging in conversation. I could still be me, but I had to bring my A game if I wanted to play real ball. I tried on my new skins—passionate *and* centered—and enjoyed elevating my entrepreneurial frequency.

Did simply changing my style and my vernacular prove myself to everyone I met from there onward? No, but it certainly helped me realize what assumptions were being made when I showed up with my fired-up, "I hope you love this idea as much as I do" presentation. It also helped me realize that I liked this person my new role was asking of me. I tried on the part of a determined, "seeking no approval because I've done the math," and full-of-heart role, and it fit me well. I didn't have to change *who* I was but *how* I channeled the excitement and love for my new work. Through the evolution, I was able to get honest with myself and realize I *had* come a long way and I *was* a lot more prepared than I realized or my saucer eyes had been suggesting. Harnessing this, I went back out into the world, welcomed all the new work that would teach me to humbly own the areas I was still learning, and showed off the aspects I'd figured out. If you haven't done it by now, do pause to reflect on how far *you've* come. More than offering some motivating perspective to embrace the work ahead, reflecting on this right now can retap your purpose and reignite your passion. I call this "spiritual surging" and it's essentially where entrepreneurs, who spend nearly all their time looking ahead or at what's right in front of them, get to truly reflect and then reconnect with their *why* and powerfully step into the present moment. Unless you get to speak at your alma mater or spend time with friends who celebrate you, pausing to look back is not natural for entrepreneurs, but it is important and jubilant. Reflect, get proud, and harness that energy into something powerful. Moving your concept from pregnancy to birth is a huge inflection point, so do connect with your spiritual side and take a moment to celebrate what brought you here and this wind-in-the-hair warrior moment!

The additional lesson here is that not everyone is going to love your ideas. And brace yourself for not everyone taking you seriously. You may not get the level of respect you might have had in the corporate world (if that's where you're coming from). In corporate settings, that annoying nine-to-five did create some structure, expectation, professional courtesy and respect, such that emails you sent yesterday were usually acknowledged by today. Yet in the entrepreneurial world, it can feel like many professionals take their sweet time getting back to you. A staggering number of entrepreneurs either back out of these processes or are unsuccessful in year one, to the tune of 90 percent, according to some sources. First-time baby business parents may feel like a dime a dozen to that graphic designer or that banker who is slow to acknowledge your inquiry, and your ego might feel a bit bruised when you have to follow up a few days later. Simply be aware of it and love it for the lesson it's teaching you in patience and accepting either the learning or the potentially better option waiting. But don't confuse waiting with passivity. You still must be active even if you're learning the timelines and rhythms of this new life. For example, let's assume you have someone to whom you've proven your seriousness. The next hurdle is to accept that you're still a number in the customer service game. And your timeline should account for this reality. At one seminar, I learned that the business community is small and to not shop around for bankers because they all talk. This was the worst advice I could have been given, because when bankers weren't taking me seriously and were moving on to bigger fish for their portfolios, I lost lots of time and a bit of my faith in professional courtesy. One time, a banker recommended by a successful independent retailer (we call it indie retailer) took six weeks to get back in touch, eventually telling me that my $90,000 loan was in fact, too small for them to work with. I hadn't wanted to shop around because of the retailer's strong endorsement, but I realized that I was just a number to the bank a few weeks in and concurrently looked for other options. While they may have considered me, I certainly wasn't thought of as a repeat customer to invest in. Had I realized this, or had they opened lines of communication with me, I could have saved a lot of time and energy. I had checked in a few times but chalked the delay up to not understanding how long processes take. I assumed they were *working*. The lesson is

---

Get used to becoming a squeaky wheel.

---

that you will have to represent your business time and time again in presentations, in trusting others and nonverbally asking others to trust you. Part of growing into your new skin is recognizing that processes or everyday courtesies may not always be in your favor, so get used to becoming a squeaky wheel and asserting the importance of your business or concept.

Stretch marks. Making it to the point where you can tell others about what's exciting you is a milestone. It means you've put in the time to gain confidence to speak about your concept-to-be and defend its honor, since no one else will prioritize it as much as you. And while it feels like another lesson in preparedness and appreciation of hard work, it's a nod to the fact that now the work is taking new shape. The parts you don't enjoy of a business startup will at times feel hefty. The act of thinking constantly about your business means your delineation of work and the rest of life will be cloudy. Still, the corner you've recently turned ushers in a new type of work that doesn't feel like work at all, at least in the beginning. These are the days when you're starting to feel squeezed but all you can think about is what life will be like when baby is here. As in, you spend all of your time picking out things for the registry and visualizing life with new purpose. As in, you're mentally becoming the mom you set out to be, and whether it be preparations that preoccupy you or figuring out what really needs to be in place for day one, you're moving in a direction of tangible creation. As in, these *are* the rewards when you're pursuing your purpose. And it feels so good! You're talking about your business and that feels good! You're developing a new vocabulary and set of skills and that feels good, too! That feeling good is exactly what your body needs during this phase of the incubation to really reenergize after all that planning. This is where the magic starts to happen. Before you know it, you'll look up from laying all these bricks and realize you have a standing business with contacts and potential customers and professionals that you worked hard for. And whether it

Application to Business

be at your first set of milestones or your hundredth, you'll draw from the same cycles of evolution. You'll get to look back on some pretty incredible creation thanks to that little bit of discomfort. You'll realize how far you've come. And you'll proudly own the feeling that you actually don't need to prove a thing at all. (Said comfortably from the more mature version to my early entrepreneurial self.) One of life's most beautiful evolutions is about to unfold.

Expect Waiting

Like many expecting mothers with their nurseries, I began imagining my storefront before knowing what the county would require of my seating plan or what expectations my landlord would have for my buildout. I studied fixtures I liked at other establishments, contemplated how the store would smell, and envisioned tickling the other senses by walking in my doors. I was off to the races, imagining the day this baby would fill more than my mind and heart space. Between imagining and talking about my business to be, I could hardly wait to bring this thing to life. Visualizing your home office as a way to recognize who you are or what you're doing helps validate your identity in this new area. It's positive, it feels great, and I encourage you to nest. The cat is out of the bag and now you're officially on a timeline, mama. But a license to nest is not a license to spend, and despite all of your best-planned designs and Pinterest posts, you have to ask yourself this question: *Is it all detailed in the financial plans?* It's handy to pull out your business plan financials and strategic plan to see what's needed (and affordable) as you start to collect resources and tools for day one. Said differently, you may have to *work* on minding your budget when the nesting kicks in, which is not as natural as one would think after belaboring all the details in the cash flow analysis. Adding an extra hard drive here or subscription there does sum quickly, and justifying purchases because "baby!" is a fast way to starve the little one, so slow yourself, sweet mama. And let's not forget you're working on your evolution, your readiness, and making sure you're setting yourself up for success.

You're working on so much that you might find that it's *all* you talk about because it's taking up so much space in your heart and mind. Totally normal, mama-to-be, but since this book is about all the ways you'll be more mindful having birthed a business, I recommend you try to find something to talk about that makes your listener feel heard, too. Not only for courtesy but also because you might learn something, shortcut some of the work, or discover a way you can work together. The advice here is to merely tune in. Be succinct and realize that even though you want to talk about this thing all the time now that you can, it's good to occasionally give yourself a break from all things business. *Especially* when you're being social with other social creatures who might need the spotlight in their direction for *who knows what* they're working through.

Learning to quiet the chatter enlivens the possibilities. It allows you to see opportunities more clearly. It, of course, evolves you. These are the stretch marks of birthing something of a sizeable nature. Like being constricted by old clothing and needing to try some maternity clothes on for size, expanding yourself to think and talk differently will come easier simply by associating with new lingo and lexicons, and a slightly different style. You will pick this up by listening and not necessarily talking. Hearing what you're supposed to be talking about is as important as telling others what you're up to. It levels up your thinking. It aligns you with bigger thoughts. Talking about "channels" and "pipelines" and "vehicles" and "margins" can surprise an old friend if they haven't heard from you in a while and surprise yourself at how much of what you focus on grows. If spending time in the business community is something you enjoy, you should start to notice some changes in your curiosity on the subject of business, as well.

Loving learning. You've heard me say a lot about embracing how you're changing and the importance of pausing and reflecting. *Application to Business*

I am belaboring the point because it really is hard to slow down when you're everything to your business. The amount of learning will continue to surprise you. Even when you think you've learned everything you can about your business, it will take on a new revenue stream or a new focus or the game will change on social media, and you get to remain a student. And student is usually synonymous with learning. And learning is strengthening. You're witnessing yourself get stronger and smarter. *It can be challenging*, but in all challenge there is growth. Getting comfortable with being a student of life and business will always serve you. *Promise.*

Expect Vulnerability and Validation Traps

Along these same lines, you'll probably start to tune in to how your level of proficiency stacks up against others. When I first realized I got a lot more out of my conversations when I listened and looked for the opportunity at play, this seeking became my new interest. Showing up as an entrepreneur but willing to welcome the unknown felt good. But if I was already depleted energetically and met many seasoned folks, I felt less proficient and realized this, too, is a fleeting experience in entrepreneurship evolution. New marketing terms or tools you haven't heard of? Realizing how little you know about tariffs that actually will affect your customer or your price? There are a zillion solutions to every single problem out there, so of course it's normal to know you don't know it all, and even if you did, options and information evolve. Stretching my old skin wasn't the issue, but getting comfortable (again) with my new skin and reaffirming (again) what a comfortable stretch felt like, was more of the work. Growth mostly felt good, but validating that I was prepared came with some work. Embracing that this kind of stretching is part of the job, each week, I set aside time for TED Talks, podcasts, or YouTube tutorials. This training proved so valuable to my own confidence and readiness that each new client I take now comes with an agreement that they give me a report each week of something they learned by exposing themselves to new topics or insights. Why? Because even if the learning comes easily in conversation, or doesn't happen naturally and requires homework, it ups your bar and makes you feel more relevant. And it is the world we exist in. Learning is breathing, and we adapt or become extinct. Plus, how good does it feel to be inspired and savvy?!

Your business with all its facets requires some learning. Much like networking, you can't dedicate all your time to leveling up your comfort, but you *can* always drop a topic into Asana that might deserve more research down the road. People love to give advice. It fills up their own buckets and makes them happy. I know this, so I ask for advice when networking to help explore a connection and usually learn something new simultaneously. In a week's time of casually asking for recommendations, I had five books and seven CRM recommendations to check out. This illustrates that you do not need to open yourself to every area where potential evolution exists, else risk reverting back to that wide-eyed and seemingly out of place business mama-to-be. Instead, consult the business plan to determine how much a recommendation plays into your priorities, research no more than three tools, pick the one with the best intersection of function, financial, and in some ways the future you (scalability), and make peace that this is the tool for the foreseeable future. When aligned with clarity, someone's book recommendation or latest cloud-based solution that isn't most relevant to your next six months need not occupy a single cell of brain space. If anyone suggests the same book or tool a second or third time, move it to the top of the list and you'll come back to it when the time is right.

Three steps. All this stretching and growing means you'll be vulnerable and will question your strength. It's a big world, and at times you won't know the right choice. Learning can be as healthy as an exercise or meditation, so add a quick five-minute YouTube video to your regimen of stretching (your body), meditat-

Application to Business

ing (your mind), and researching (your readiness) each morning. Five minutes in each bucket means that fifteen minutes into your working day you can feel educated, prepared, and confident . . . and squeezing out doubt. In my experience, decisions then came more naturally. Sure, I had to catch up on the news using an app such as theSkimm instead of reading the complete newspaper, but this was my trade-off, and it quieted the questions and overwhelm I could easily feel. And, bonus of five minutes in the buckets that mattered to me, I strengthened my sense of self and that *I'm doing my best* feeling in the business real world.

Expect Dividends on Your Pitch

Faking it till you make it is a real strategy and is used just about everywhere, *by everyone*. Being knowledgeable and ready is a relative term, anyway. Everyone has room for a bit of growth in every department, and the sooner that's accepted, the faster we can carry on with achieving. Still, even with a lot of practice, my first elevator pitch was something closer to three minutes and probably lost my audience somewhere around the fourth or fifth floor. Even with planning and sketching, I led with what it was and not why it mattered, because my concept was difficult to explain! *Rookie move.* But proving I had a special something to offer the world absolutely started with the elevator pitch, and that meant I had to exude confidence, tell the story, be relevant by creating curiosity, and get them to care about what I had to say—*all in the same setting . . . and amidst other strangers sometimes listening in . . . and with zero cares that I'm naturally a shy person.* That's pressure! But I focused on being relevant and harnessed what I observed in other effective business mamas and found what I needed to do: I needed to hook them in the first ten seconds so they actually listened to the remaining twenty. This stacks up with the adage that you have "seven seconds to make a first impression." As mentioned in chapter 2, learning what it took to engage someone in ten seconds, not thirty, also potentially afforded some space to garner questions and in turn learn something from someone else instead of exclusively selling myself. This fixed all the other pressurized elements of being relevant in thirty seconds right up. I left room for them to actually decide to care, because I took care in ensuring a conversation rather than a spiel.

Being succinct in my elevator pitch went beyond gaining a customer or mentor. It allowed me to move into opportunities to collaborate, share enthusiasm, and take advantage of a chance to learn in the moment. Relating to the listener *in the first ten seconds* before their mind wanders back to whatever is more pressing—their own business, their actual babies, and so on—can open you to compounded benefits from thinking about your business not in a vacuum but in relation to the world around you. Your continued conversation relies on your being succinct and agile to apply to your audience at hand. My elevator pitch generally went like this:

"Have you ever wanted a place to just relax and quickly step away from your day? Well that's what I'm working on with House of Steep by helping busy people feel more connected to their lives—we're doing it over tea, foot soaks, and reflexology/foot massage."

Even if that's not your (ahem) cup of tea, you're intrigued and might even volley back a few questions. Score! They'll remember you even more now that they're engaged. Depending on who I was talking to, I might add a call to action like, "it's a great option for date night," or "I hope you'll follow us for some tasting events we have planned" but usually after giving them a chance to react. *Important note: I didn't pitch this way on an actual elevator—on elevators I'd lead in with "thank goodness for elevator rides to slow us down a little . . ." and from there we see if the conversation allowed for me to talk about my new way to relax.*

Seasoned entrepreneurs will refine their pitch to attract a different audience as the business cycles go on, so your pitch will continue to grow as you do. I joined a local woman entrepreneur networking group where we saw a lot of the same faces. I found myself refining my pitch each month to stay relevant. I got a lot of customers from this circle, so saying the same thing each time risked my getting tuned out. Sometimes I really needed them to know not that I was still there for their one-on-one meetings but that we were seeing a lot of traction in our baby showers or corporate events, to plant a seed for them to think about us differently. In fact, in a different accountability group I joined, we purposely changed our pitch to have an arsenal of ways to think about different audiences. Since no two people are alike, it is helpful not only to practice the timing of your pitch but also the lead-in and hooks.

This whole exercise applies to your need to draw on your flexibility and ability to shed tendencies or skins that don't serve you in the business world . . . *like shyness. . . . or an ability to run away with my thoughts or go off on tangents . . . about myself . . . or that car that just drove by. . . . you get the point.* Here again, addressing this awareness sharpens your mindfulness practices alongside your business mom evolutions. Ask yourself "what does success look like if I'm relating to my audience?" and then look for those signs when pitching. If you feel energized coming out of a conversation but you could tell you lost them in the back half of your pitch, you know it's time for a change. Through mindfulness, you'll learn to recognize the times you'll need to relate, the times to simply listen to another entrepreneur's pitch, and the times to adapt. Resilience comes with your practice of being relevant to your listener and the creativity you apply to entering a conversation.

In summary, all that you can expect in the early moments is very personal. Everything is for the health of the baby—your decisions, your focus, your objective for inner peace—all of it. Feeling more stress about the financial aspects of your personal and business well-being is also normal now that all you think about is business. Your focus can get stronger, especially now that the news is out and the drive to thrive has kicked in. You're naturally expanding through your loving focus. This focus will turn into the milk that will fuel your baby. Natural growing pains around the topic are healthy, so try to welcome them for the future life they fortify.

Expecting: Going Public

Business ownership still is fun, and the scary parts do normalize with practice.

Once you've put it out there though, the pressure is on. Mostly from yourself but potentially from others. Plan to start small. A lean startup mentality will help your learning curve and your own expectations.

▶ Hooking people is exciting. Seeing them engage is enlivening. Have fun with that part, too.

▶ Don't forget to reflect.

▶ Love your own shifts as a result of getting the word out.

☐ Your Readiness Journal

If you haven't done so yet, now is a great time to work on your mission and values alongside your elevator pitch with this deeper work happening as a result of your coming out

_____

_____

_____

_____

_____

_____

_____

_____

_____

Now with this space, list ten people you can practice on and get solid feedback from. Then list ten places you plan to go public with your own message.

1 _____

2 _____

3 _____

4 _____

5 _____

6 _____

7 _____

8 _____

9 _____

10 _____

5

Forward Momentum

Expect Engagement

In the beginning, I had all my social platforms and the website set up to alert me anytime I got a new follower or subscriber. Talk about glorious feels! Anytime these little gems punctuated my day, it meant there were *actual people* out there willing to invest their precious time and attention in following my progress. And when celebrities (okay, bloggers) or personalities with lots of followers began finding me, I was over the moon. These little "kicks" happen just at the right time to counterbalance the less glamorous milestones along the way . . . like, closing out your first month on QuickBooks. These small-but-*will*-be-celebrated victories are an antidote to the scary mornings when you have no idea where to start, or the ominous cloud that descends when you haven't seen a single click on that campaign you worked so hard on. I encourage you to practice celebrating—as in *really enjoying*—the small victories. These are the kicks that remind you why you're doing this, even if they do make it hard to sleep.

Like all experiences good or less than good, here they are, and you get to *choose* to use them to help propel you or simply amuse you. *I suggest the former.* It's no doubt this period will be hard. You have a business and you're seeing nuggets of validation for what you're creating, yet it may very well be the hardest you've worked for something you can't see or really feel yet. But those small rewarding kicks can balance your experience and punctuate the harder times. However, they will only get you so far in the beginning; as you crank up for more challenges, directly correlated does the reward size need to be. There will come a time you need to turn off the reminders and power through the parenting, for instance graduating your focus into deeper work like nurturing genuinely curious prospects into signed contracts of customers who will rave about you. Right about when you're enjoying the satisfaction of checking your metrics is exactly the time to look for new milestones and measures for growth. Complacency won't get you there, but looking high and digging in deep, will.

Growing and nurturing the victories in this example means engaging authentically with your audience. Engaging early not only helps build loyal followers, it also connects you to your mission in a way that aligns with our human nature, not to mention keeping the love (ahem, cash) flowing to your business. We are social creatures and, like it or not, we respond to validating cues from others on how meaningful our offering is to them. Engaging authentically assumes you've already figured out where your customers already are (Pinterest, Facebook, email). Then what you share, which doesn't have to be original content, speaks to some need on their level. If they have kids and your business is about something very different (let's say your business is art procurement), think about a common theme. Rich experiences come to mind, so share content about that. It's important to also share information that helps explain what you do or how you can help someone who didn't know they needed your help. And giving in this way will help both parties feel more connected. They may be surprised to see a businessperson talking about things other than their company. This surprise factor will spike their curiosity and get them thinking about you as a dynamic, likable person they want to support. If you can't find a common theme for external content, think about what your voice is (and, invariably, what your company's voice is) and share accordingly. For my first business, my personality shone through to my posts and newsletters, and people loved them. It was a playful, "did ya know" and "sharing is caring" tone that spoke from my heart and resonated well with followers who were all trying to do the best for their health or families but also trying not to take themselves so seriously. Finding your voice will help you connect with your readers. Being consistent and thoughtful will help the rest of the interaction, which will include keeping their interest, teaching them something, and/or inspiring them to stay in touch for more. This level of engagement will help them build a connection to you and your business early on.

There is a second part to engaging authentically, and that's being responsive. It's one thing to be thoughtful about what you put out, but you must be willing to lovingly support any feedback you get, whether it be in follows, likes, or comments. Now, there is a whole etiquette around each tool and what's appropriate (following back, responding within twenty-four hours, etc.) and there are also quirks to tools, like shadow branding limitations, so get comfortable with the knowledge that none of the vehicles are perfect, and some of them might not be a fit for you and your audience. But being responsive means more than saying thank you if someone appreciates your post. It's gesturing that you're committed to the same things they care about. It's agreeing or politely disagreeing and keeping the conversation going so everyone can feel heard. Imagine they're in front of you, and respond the way you would if you were having the conversation over coffee. Rather than "thanks, hope to see you over on my live feed tonight," try to weave in the "what's next" with some form of genuine gratitude and why it really matters that you can talk to them. Instead, try, "I sincerely hope to keep this energy going over on the live feed tonight. Thanks for taking the time to engage," or "It would mean so much to have your feedback on my blog post tomorrow; I write content for people just like you and would love to know if I'm still hitting the mark," or something along these lines.

Finally, you can engage authentically by being a reliable source. If you tell them they'll hear from you monthly via newsletter, make that a priority. Even if they don't read it, knowing that you're there helps their subconscious trust and helps your credibility. Commit to a "relationship" you can manage. If you can only post and be responsive once a day, do that. If you can only come up with unique content once a month, do that. Whatever you do, do it with both your business *and* their interests in mind, otherwise you will only be pushing your agenda, and while that is important at various intervals, it is not what will develop loyal followers who want to refer their friends to you.

If you're having trouble figuring out what this looks like, go ahead and stalk your inspiration business—the company you want yours to grow to be. You'll get a lot of ideas by looking around, and while you cannot copy verbatim, it's pretty common to "borrow" promotional ideas or styles. I would recommend that if you do recycle, try to look for a company outside your immediate industry who does it well but wouldn't be a business your customer might also be following. The downside of leveraging others for inspiration is that you could become stale to your customer, so skillfully consider where you seek inspiration. Would a Guy Fawkes Day sale seem fitting for your cheeky business, too? Give it a try if it makes sense for your customer. It's completely normal to study other business bellies, but a word of caution is to not go around comparing yours to others. Baby creation comes in all shapes and sizes and you can't possibly compare your efforts to grow the healthiest business baby to anyone else of different means, timelines, and resources.

Expect Improvement

When I was busy planning out blog posts for the month, I realized that I was duplicating work across my newsletter, blog, and then social media posts. The need for a system to better connect my tools became paramount when I also needed to include more stakeholders: my team in the store handling promotions, our graphic designer aligned with marketing collateral, the staff who handled the newsletter, and of course me, doing many of the social posts. Even before I had the team, I still needed a way to automate processes and not recreate the wheel each time. I looked at the vehicles I had chosen and who I needed to reach. I sorted which could be identical to text on the blog and newsletter, and where some finessing was required. What ended up being born in this early time was a process of how I went about marketing, as well as a flow chart on how I would share content. It was a lifesaver when it came time to post again the next year, by not recreating the wheel on seasonal promotions and sharing articles that were still relevant. I was able to look back holistically to see what composition inspired the most readers and where evergreen content could emerge or solidify.

Sample Marketing Plan

Hug Factory Roadmap

January	February	March	April	May	June	July	August	September	October	November	December
Brand Management											
	Print Collateral: New Menus			Print Collateral: Info Rack			Print Collateral: Design			Print Collateral: Referral Cards	
	Booth School Fair			Booth Runners Event				Booth TBD Smart Target			Booth Craft Fair
Neighbor business cookie/card drop						Neighbor business cookie/card drop					
Promotions											
						Google Key Word Campaign					
Yelp ad campaign									Holiday gift card promo		
		Partnership Program with Priority Charity					Partnership Program with Priority Charity			Small Biz Saturday	
	Our favorite month promo				Sale						
Education/Content											
Blog: S.A.D	Blog: Love	Blog: Dopamine	Blog: Pheromones	Blog: Law of Attraction	Blog: Compassion	Blog: Kid Summer	Blog: Charity	Blog: Cortisol	Blog: Healing touch	Blog: Oxytocin	Blog: Stress Mgt
		Seminar: Self Esteem			Seminar: Overcoming Grumpiness				Seminar: Nutrition Correlaries		
Weekly Meditation Talks - world influences, effects on mind and body, importance of regular practice, reflections on impact, styles of meditation and auyrveda's role in focus and successfully interacting with thoughts.											
Channel Maintenance											
Co-space: Chair Massage	Campaign: Community of One (neighbor business)					Co-Space: Longevity/Life		Postcard campaign - 2 mile	Co-Space: Chiro Talk		
	Reach New Target (nursing homes)							Reach New Target (moms groups)		Donations: PTA Auction	
Share, Blog spotlight, Exclusive Follower Perks											

Built from list of ideas (compiled throughout year). These priorities have space to execute, rather than list of things that compound on top of each other. Consider program maintenance before layering in new ideas.

Decide on when marketing reviews will be (monthly, quarterly)

I was also able to hand this off to a marketing intern for baseline, and created a little space in my own head knowing I would always start with the blog and those links would then spur newsletter and social posts for the month, then lastly the marketing collateral. Just having this system in place and working meant more space for creativity and enjoying the good feelings about the path I was on.

Systems are so helpful. *Timesaving, decision-minimizing, shortcutting marvels to help keep you grounded.* Yet any don't-know-what-you-don't-know entrepreneur will tell you that what worked in the beginning likely isn't the tool you're wildly successful with. But it starts with having systems that you can evolve down the road, so the message here is that if you're going to have a mind for growth (read *change*), it's always healthy to check back in on a system or tool that's meant to help. If your goals change, so might the process to achieve them. In my experience, many systems initialized at the beginning had a shelf life, even if it was selected with an eye to scale. Most of these decisions are made on a shoestring when starting up, and that's absolutely okay. Spreadsheets instead of project management tools are totally great. Keep using any system that keeps you in flow. And if there is a sense that when the volume is turned up a notch that spreadsheet won't address your highest functioning needs, first, take pride in yourself for thinking agilely. Then, make a note on your strategic plan. The tool you choose today should be a nice segue into the future tool, with the time between being the elements that help you learn what else you need for success after building a business around your plans (and little cash). Ahh, the plans. It's great to have a plan. It's great to have monthly goals that tie back to your plan. It's great to find yourself in good habits of quarterly evaluation when the quarters feel like days and the days like minutes. Time will speed and, similar to getting on daycare lists in advance when all signs are pointing to healthy baby arrival, solving problems today that satisfy some baseline expectation in the future is gratifying. For me, I knew I eventually wanted to invest in a better CRM system, but the budget wouldn't allow in the early days. It was still too early to layer it in, but I really started figuring out which functionalities I would need once time and success were under my belt, and I began adding those details to my customer tracking spreadsheet. Note: With the technology available today, spreadsheets in lieu of CRMs is not an approach I recommend. Many CRM solutions have a free or nearly free entry point, so don't be intimidated if you can't afford what some business owners can. They all started somewhere (without a lot of fungible cash), so think bigger and settle on a tool that can get you there without a lot of overhauls. The reason I mention it here is that it's a good inflection point now that things are starting to get real, if you recognize that spreadsheets or systems might be hard to maintain when the customers are your focus, and refreshing documents or processes are somewhere on your distant to-do list.

Expect Devotion

While having rewards fueled energy, the rosy picture I painted is punctuated with the thorns of reality. Getting some followers and interest helped me feel *slightly* less nauseous about the investment I was making in a retail space. At the time, I had no idea of what a proper timeline would be. I've learned in the work I do now that there are typical arrival schedules but no true timelines that apply to all businesses. Generally speaking, I was moving at a moderate pace, working through whatever the day presented. But once I was feeling the kicks, my nesting instinct deepened and I knew I had to get serious about securing my retail space, and serious about what the future held. Saying no to book club and saying yes to intimidating contracts was the new black. The time of no turning back was now, and I needed to start doing some very serious things. *Just like that.*

Actually, not just like that. Because there was all of that learning to get to this point. But pre-contract and post-contract life does feel like some magnificent shift to the speed of time. However, speeding into contracts is the last thing you should do. Signing a contract is the best way to put you on a fast track to launching your business, so trust your gut on timing of contracts. Factor in what you can lovingly commit to *right now*, decide what you'll be able to afford energetically and financially, now and in the future. Negotiate your best-case scenario, like rent abatement on your pop-up space or deferred commencement on your work office, if applicable, that look out for the unknown. At some point you need to make a decision and sign some contracts, but always calculate if holding off a bit longer is an option. Listen to your gut. If risk is low or you absolutely know this is the deal for you from multiple angles, go ahead and sign for an agreement that puts you on a reasonable timeline. This goes for lining up helpers if your business requires hands and making sure you're secure with the *how* of the future. Approach change with a spirit of exploration. Be willing to fail to see what happens if the stakes are lower. Scientifically, if you're doing your purpose, you're already more productive, which can lead to results just in the doing.

Application to Business

Know your needs. If you're still currently employed and don't intend to work part-time while launching, now might be a good time to consider developing your exit strategy from the day job. While some business models are more forgiving than others, ultimately this is the first of many big, balanced decisions you are rewarded with making! One of my lessons learned is that I quit my job too early, and I wished I had realized the things I could be doing (read: costs that needed funding) while still earning a paycheck. But there are many who argue they wouldn't have ever launched if they didn't pull the trigger.

Real-Life Example

Even the late Kate Spade regretted for a minute leaving her job in haste when she decided to trade it all in for her boxy burlap handbag design. She had a product that was interesting but no business experience to help her trust the future of no medical benefits or promise of income to pay for, you know, food. She quickly acknowledged that her exit was hasty, but it made her hungry. And resourceful. A close friend later reminded her that her newfound scrappiness and determination were necessary to get her company off the ground, so the timing of her drastic leap was perfect. Your exit is hopefully somewhere between the place of readiness and financial comfort to take the risk. And sign no contract before you're in a place that makes perfect sense for you, your food and shelter, and the needs of your baby business to be.

Expecting: Forward Momentum

The small rewards are awesome, but strive for the deeper rewards of gaining contacts through adding value. These are the real moments that build this experience.

Try not to compare your belly to others. Rather, use interactions with more seasoned parents to fuel you.

Best-laid plans are silly. But try your best to lay them anyway and then detach from the outcome. You're exactly where you're supposed to be.

☐ Your Readiness Journal

What do you want from this period? Is it energy, wisdom, growth? Set your intention clearly and set your goals accordingly.

_____

_____

_____

_____

_____

_____

_____

Think about exploring what your goals could be for the rest of the year. They can be placeholders now, but go ahead and make room for them as you think about your timeline. After setting your goals, it's important to really stand back and think about if that's truly what you want. Growth might be what the world thinks makes sense, but does that path get you something? The goals need to make sense for you, too.

6

Final Preparations

Expect Getting Away

You know the feeling when you didn't know how thirsty you were until you took that first sip? Or that satiated feeling when you *finally* get what you were asking for, and it hits the spot? A more perfect analogy couldn't be made for the feeling when I took an unscheduled leave. By this time, I had been executing my startup plans, having more high-impact conversations (good, and also hard), and thinking through every little detail all day and all night. I wasn't tired; I was high on energy from simply working on my personal mission. If left to my own devices, I probably wouldn't have looked up anytime in the near future because of all the work, and of course, all the feels. But my future self knew that if that level of intensity were to continue, I would need to take a little break, and that's exactly where I landed.

My dear friend was moving across the country, and while ten days seemed excessive, I agreed to a little life spice and drove her from DC to San Francisco. It was amazing, of course. The open road does bring perspective in how vast the world is and the possibilities it holds. We didn't talk too much about the business but rather the way life unravels. We made funny car videos of us lip-syncing to our favorite songs and posted them on social media. We had the best time being free, our friends cheered us on as we took a pause before our lives became very different, and we connected with carefreeness and bliss.

The best part of the impromptu adventure is that I didn't know how badly I needed it until it was in front of me, waving the once-in-a-lifetime banner. If I didn't go, I would regret it, and besides, I had no real commitments since I had quit my job too early, my marriage hit a rough patch from putting our savings on the line, and my new "investor" husband was wanting to know how I was spending my time. I was feeling the pressure to perform from both self and spouse, and I recognized I was really pushing myself to power through. But not realizing how fast I was running toward this budding business (and away from life) became apparent with a little space from the planning. I couldn't help it; the business was adorable and I couldn't stop loving on it, and it loved me back in the right ways, even before it was born. But the periods of pressure or bliss are both times to take a break to appreciate more what is in front of you, recognize your depths, and gain the perspective of what deeper could look like. So, a babymoon I took, and never regretted stepping away. Clarity I could never have gained in my usual routine became evident in my choosing working on the business over working on my relationship. Clarity when I couldn't get lost in the *doing* happened when I felt how deep the love for the life I was about to embark on had become. If you can't manage a trip, meaningfully remove yourself from your business for at least a week before you launch. This kind of sabbatical is a requirement for anyone on the brink of launching something new. Period.

Breaks: 1,000 percent necessary. It's no news that stepping away helps productivity, and it's certainly no news that you're going to need to recharge when you are the only driving force behind your business. Batteries recharge, and so do people. It's hard to get it in the moment, but set a reminder on your calendar if need be. Take that break, if for nothing else than to truly measure how badly you needed it. Your business and creative space will bow to you as you honor yourself, and you'll get to recognize how much more power you can create versus using your reserves to muscle through.

Expect New Resolve

Fear is one of the strongest pulls known to the human experience. Our brains are *wired* to be fearful. Sure, fear is here to make the next time easier as you evolve, but it's when you turn the corner of homestretch that a brand-new level of terror takes residence in your mind space. Taking out a loan is scary, but nothing's more alarming than committing to how you'll spend that money. I hired five people before I earned a penny of storefront revenue that would hopefully justify their cost. The feeling that the cash would never be seen until I made some money was heavy. If self-doubt hadn't slowed this entrepreneur down to date, hiring staff and paying vendors for raw goods welcomed nervous energy right on my doorstep. I had figured out how to identify fear and other emotions that would surface throughout the months leading up to this pivot, but the thoughts and feelings of permanency were new. And suffocating. And scary. I couldn't breathe through them as easily because there was no rationalizing them away. It's a change. A big one. And the weight of it then becomes familiar and quickly returns with future shifts. I walked around with that burden for almost a week before I realized how its heft was harming my productivity. I was only able to shake it after acknowledging that this is what I wanted. Maybe I didn't appreciate the impact, but it was part and parcel with the goal. I chose this heft. *Anything that was there was my own and I welcomed it.* And I stepped through the weight with the prayer that this beautiful, living thing would serve me more than it scared me. Now, my resolve was fluid and would move from time to time. Sometimes I had my sights on awakening through this, and sometimes I had my sights on eventually having a partner to share some of the responsibility. Or maybe investors to take some of the financial pressure off once I had something tangible. Or many other potential exits that didn't sound so bad when I worked through them.

Whatever is coming up for moms when the end/beginning is near, it too can pass. Everything, in fact, does pass. Thoughts are just thoughts and you get to choose what you do with them. Remember also the tools for making choices from chapter 2 (will this matter in three minutes, three months, three years) are easy ways to move past fears at the end of your pre-child era. Thinking or ruminating thoughts are defenses to embracing the emotion of fear. Truly feeling the fear will help you better manage it when it comes up again.

Application to Business

It's all normal. Fears around big decisions are completely normal, especially hiring and signing contracts for the first time. Looking on the bright side, going through the process of interviewing can be gratifying if you're finding people who are qualified, and bring you peace of mind that you can grow this thing. If decisions become consuming, the good news is that there are business doulas who can guide you through your birthing process. When you're prospering, hiring team members is an option, too. If your worst fears do materialize, there's usually someone who can help you. If pennies are stretched, hopefully the book you're holding can serve as your compass of hope coming from someone who has been there and still successfully achieved the sale of her first business. Trepidation and protection of your resources is normal, so trust that you will make balanced decisions.

If hiring is in your plan, this stage in business incubation is an excellent time to be hiring, and I encourage you to review the interview questions in this book (chapter 2) and on the website www.lyndseydepalma.com.

Timeline Tip

Expect Prayer and Mantra

Be it through self-motivated, outsourced, or business birth–coach help, if you're at this place, your delivery date is near! For the bulk of my experience, I was frontloading as much as I could because of the ill-timed departure from my career. I was prepared with employee manuals created, onboarding checklists, and contracts prepared, but suddenly I felt like there was an abyss between me and actually delighting customers with delicious tea and rich experiences. Once the start was near, I was moving fast. The work quickly shifted to getting the space situated, tables ordered, inventory organized, staff interviewed, and developing a whole new list of things I simply had not thought of until this point. While I had tested my POS system and thought about how fast I needed the transactions to go through, I hadn't really given much thought to functional layout of the place, or where I was going to store certain things now that I saw how much space two pounds of tea took up. Or, now that I had all of these things accepted into inventory, what ways I needed to load them into the POS system to track raw goods in the ways I'd be serving the tea. I learned that a whole new wave of to-dos can creep up on you that even the most thoughtful planner may not have fully anticipated. And those to-dos needed to be done yesterday! Even if you're launching an online business or a consulting company, your instinct to nest will move to a frenetic pace as your due date approaches. I was busy tending to not only my old loose ends but brand-new loose ends when my contractor showed up and said, "Congratulations, you're open for business" as he held out my certificate of occupancy. In that moment, the lists were as heavy as a boulder. No approval process or vendor to blame. *I* was the thing standing in the way of my doors opening, and it was me and my lists looking at each other with judgey eyes.

Earlier that morning I had been busy telling interviewees we'd be open in a few weeks, yet we could technically be open tomorrow. Enter the weight of the world. Or at least of all those people who had been asking when I would finally be open (eighteen months of hopeful "could be next month!" people). I had gotten so used to the "almost!" fable that I didn't realize how much I had distanced myself from the possibility of making money on this concept. When it was here, I was paralyzed.

Sure, there had been some early contractions, but there is nothing on earth like when the This. Is. Real moment hits. The tools I finally decided on after demoing for months, the nice cardstock for the brochures, putting a deposit down for the first trade show or fair. The big investments don't mean there is no turning back, but they do mean there is only one way to see any return on them and that's through this thing. The water has broken. This is it. Ready or not, life as you know it is changing. Some babies come on their own schedule. Some moms are fortunate enough to dictate when that baby makes its debut. A well-planned, intentionally timed gestation and beautifully launched business still needs to shift to doing business. For any type of launch, you're more prepared than your perfectionism is probably letting you think. You want to launch ninety days out from Valentine's Day to sell your cake pops. That makes sense. You want to launch your tea shop in the fall so people remember you when they need something to do when the weather gets cold. That makes sense. You want to start making money as soon as practically possible, yet a few client testimonials could make the difference for your splash. A soft opening to trial some clients likely makes sense. The way it is pictured is probably not precisely how it will come to pass, but everyone gets to have their own version of their birth story. You may have pictured the birth over and over and believe me, there's real power to visualizing it: the official email to your colleagues asking them to share the word, pushing Go

> *There is nothing on earth like when the This. Is. Real moment hits.*

on your ecommerce link, or leaving your cards on a popular community board for the world to see . . . it's there and picturable. It's easy to dream of unicorn launches of a business, but ultimately the goal is delivery, and no one is going to tell you that you missed the mark when it's your vision that only you can see. And similar to breathing through a real birth, it's important to have a list of mantras for the tougher moments:

▶ Respond not react; look at things sans emotion

▶ Is this a make or buy decision; sometimes it can be black and white

▶ See the lesson, not the inadequacy; judgment is so not helpful in this fledgling state

▶ No mud, no lotus: only in hard times can you find your depths

▶ Anything that helps you feel the feeling but doesn't take you offline completely

It's helpful to remember that you're the only person positioned to bring this baby to life, and that became a mantra for me when the decisions were tough or the fears were strong. *I am the best mom for this business.* And so it went.

The way through is through. Even though fear (perhaps pure terror) is a huge part of these moments, gently remind yourself *Application to Business* that deep inside, this is exactly what you were seeking and it's just part of the process. You're contracting (literally and proverbially), you're overcoming fears, you're recognizing the magnitude of this thing, for better or for worse. But don't close your eyes to get through it. Feel yourself wondering if you really knew how much this was or what this really meant, and wonder whether if you knew the answer you'd still change anything. Invigorating or intimidating, it's here. Ground with what you want out of this business. Narrow in on what rewards look like and what is reality. Trust that it's going to be one memorable trip.

I had the biggest "come to mama" moment in my professional life the last night before my doors were "gently" opened. I had told the world I could do something bold, and I had laid some serious groundwork to get to this point. I had posted "tomorrow's the day" to the followers who immediately began cheering me on. Tomorrow's opening was dictated by a customer who had reached out asking if I could please be the destination where she and her sisters could celebrate her birthday. I had said yes, but with the understanding that I may need to ask for forgiveness as we practiced on her and her siblings. But that advance permission still didn't help calm my nerves when so much work had come down to what would unfold a few hours from then. I was cheering myself on, but all alone in the dimly lit storefront I was about to open, I felt really alone. Sitting on top of the tea bar, in the silence of the furnished store, I had my biggest freak-out to date. I had no one but myself to catch me if I fell off that bar . . . or cheer me. It was too late to call anyone to get their encouragement or understanding. There was me, with no net, and I was about to take the biggest leap of my life. The blood had all but left my head when I realized this was it. Instinctually, because I had practiced this a few times, I reminded myself of the *why* I had told so many people in my elevator pitch. *I am* the woman for the job. It's in *my* DNA. We *need* this. I

moved my laptop out of my lap and looked around, like I would do thousands of times from that day forth, and said a simple yes. This *is* the time and I *will* move mountains.

I looked up and saw the reflection of my window decal logo (three tea cups and a leaf) projected on the wall. I said hello to my newly revealed effigy "steaming leaf," and went home and tried to sleep.

Expecting: Final Preparations

▶ Take a perspective trip, for at least a day, forcing you away from your laptop so you can breathe the needed life into this thing.
▶ Create your list of mantras for confidence and tools for embodying your new life, and tattoo them in your office or on your mirror.
▶ You can shift the internal and it does shift the external.
▶ Every time we see a difficulty through to the other side, we've created space and that thing won't scare us as much.

□ Your Readiness Journal

V isualize your launch, in words and in pictures.

_____

_____

_____

_____

_____

_____

_____

Has your model shifted at all now that you're thinking through the emotional realities of the plans you laid?

Part III

The Launch, Lessons,
and Loving Your Gorgeous Creation

7

Birthing Your Business: Precious *and* Painful

Expect Oxygen

Being the gentle but unstoppable "steaming leaf" meant that I rolled into my shop at 5 a.m. daily, three hours before the doors were due to open. I was only getting about four hours of sleep because I was so energized by the tasks to address, and I was staying up far too late . . . I couldn't help myself. I was spinning in circles, jumping from partially completed task to partially completed task because this was one deadline that needed *all* of my focus. In college, I could buckle down and get to the finish line. This launch was the deepest line I'd ever seen, and there were a thousand things that stood between me and crossing it, mostly in the name of perfection. I felt my chest tightening but wasn't sure whether it was from excitement or overwhelm or both. I organized and reorganized things that were definitely not on my list but somehow felt important in those moments because right then, even though I knew better, *everything* mattered. My friends were texting me well wishes. My landlord stopped in to buy a cup of tea so he could donate his dollar change to signify my first sale. I don't think I took a breath for three hours. Then my first employee, Karen, showed up. Her aura is so kind and loving, and she reminded me that no one I was about to meet really knew what to expect. She was so right. It was such a unique concept and they would be more curious than anything. They hadn't seen the business plan nor heard me mull over the vision and what it was supposed to be. So I sat myself at the corner table and looked at what they might experience. I had a clean space, delicious tea, and a memorable experience to offer them. I took a deep breath and exhaled into the concept . . . and I was open for business.

I didn't realize how caught up in perfection I really had become until those last few days. Thankfully, I was able to reject the fears of never being successful and reconnect with what I was here to do: provide a safe place for people to relax. Provide a home for people to become aware of their bodies, stresses, and ways they could be nurtured. Make enough money to pay the beautiful souls who were so thrilled to be a part of this. Nurture myself to make sound, grounded decisions and be present to show up for whatever the moment called for. So, with a reconnection to my mission and the love this creation was intended to share, I was able to send some of that love back. I opened the doors and made my first push for sales.

Application to Business

Phoning home. I knew recalibrating back toward center would happen, but I didn't expect it to happen so soon. Or so often. There is a reason why business owners print their values and mission statements on their real estate. It's not only for the customers, it's for the business. Even if you think you won't need a reminder of who you are, when catching sight of your mission statement and thinking about the feeling or place you were in when choosing a particular word in it, you may realize that you've drifted away. If you want to practice coming back to that place full of heart and vision, focus on that same meaningful word choice and apply it to business problems. Connecting with home, you'll always find your way.

Expect Release

My birth story was more revealing than I expected:

Hour 1   the floodgates of reality, with only a handful of customers but at least ten sticky notes per hour of supplies we'd need (more thermometers and mixing bowls and dishwashing gloves and . . .).

Hour 3   a new sticky was created for things that I needed before close of business, much less before we opened the next day (more cash for the cash drawer, because even for a heavy credit card business, five transactions will crush your supply of small bills).

Hour 5   a little clarity that I would need a folder (added to my list) or a daily log planner to put these notes in.

Hour 7   lovingly joked with customers about best-laid plans and better shoes.

Hour 9   sent staff home halfway through the closing process, largely so I could collapse on the sanctuary chairs in privacy; having staff see me weak was nothing my ego would allow, at least not then.

I pushed all day long and came close to tears a few times, purely from exhaustion. The risers for the sanctuary chairs were already bending, my lists were long or misplaced, and I had gone back to the mental drawing board on processes and flow of customers more than my tired brain could handle. Yet I looked down at the app that tracked our revenue, and we had exceeded our revenue target and were pushing people out the doors an hour past closing time. We had made a lot of people so happy, including my own sleepy soul. I stood back from my sweet new baby business and felt even more certain of my purpose. After taking a step back, the list that seemed overwhelming was but a road map of new ways to lovingly serve the business, and the other pre-launch lists were proving relatively unimportant now that I had lived a day in the life of my business. There were still many unknowns, but by simply having done, a light was shone through and delivered confidence that I could address everything that came with looking my baby business in the eyes for the first time.

Six hours before the launch I was running around, trying to figure out what else I could do to help the cause. I knew I couldn't be 100 percent ready, and I knew there would need to be room to learn. All of this made sense on a cognitive level. Viscerally, however, I could barely stomach the thought of another list of things to tend to, until I *had* that third list of actually living the dream, now called the living list and replacing the others I had created to date. There will surely be surprises whether it be in your lists, your observation of your mindset, or others' reaction to your offering. That's normal and makes your birth story unique. But one theme ribbons through every birth memoir, which is that none of them are ever as prescribed or planned. Not control, but rather, calling deep on your soul teaches your body to strap in for the ride. Maybe you expect sales right away, but perhaps that's not your destiny today. Maybe you sign a big deal and it goes better than expected. No matter what, by opening your business, you've opened yourself to the deepest well of learning (tactically, spiritually, emotionally, and physically), and you are officially positioning yourself to monetize your capabilities in a brand-new way. *Bottom line.*

Pure and simple. The feeling of doing and achieving may blur together, and this is normal. Staring at what you've created is absolutely normal. Finding reasons to reread a complimentary *Application to Business* email from a customer is in fact helpful. Ignoring friends, family, and life so you can revel in how this feels is reasonable in this sweet period with your new marvel. Just remember, there are only a few needs this baby has in the beginning. As a business, it doesn't even need food and warmth. It simply needs to fill your soul and pay for itself. That is it, and all you need to align with. The impulse is often to give away merchandise, free time, and focus on low-hanging fruit on your to-do list. These things all serve your exhaustion but don't necessarily get you to a place where you're not nurturing this thing day and night. People don't have babies for them to stay babies and to stay in the fog of earlydom forever. Find ways to reward yourself daily as a way to replenish your energy bank, and train your sight on what clarity can and will feel like when you're not in the weeds of new business ownership. Set goals that allow you to interact with your business baby in a way that feeds a bond. Practice is how you keep feeding yourself, whichever method does the trick for you. It's not selfish; it's necessary. Your baby wants to grow, and extracting positive rewards is a way to be in a healthy place as you both develop into your roles. Carefully studying the business's evolution and livelihood is a lot like gawking at your creation, but it will smile back eventually. Let that be a reminder to you to stand back for some larger perspective.

Expect Oneness

That first transitional period of replacing earlier lists with the "in practice" punch list can be considered an omen. There are things that you *want* for the business (like a playlist or automated check-in process) and then there are surprises and important implementations that you *need* for your business. Having a label system for tea orders by the ounce (to consume at home) was somewhere in a distant cloud of future notions, but not anticipating the volume of customers who wanted to take tea home with them after drinking, a system to identify what's in the take-home pack (and the FDA's subsequent labeling requirements) ensued. The acceptance of the preparations that readied me for some things—but certainly not for all—allowed me to sink into a sense of oneness with my business. *I couldn't possibly have planned for it all.* The future will teach you that there are more things you want or could do for your business than there are actual hours in the day. Realizing what I thought my business needed was not what it desired was tough because I thought I knew best. But I demoted my ego and the old list items to low priority; I'd get to them when the baby napped. But for now, I would respond to baby business woes, and baby would smile. I would trust that connection as a guide that would let my mind rest just a bit.

The care and feeding of a business doesn't happen by checking boxes alone. Ideas will come and go, and acting on them doesn't necessarily mean the problem is solved. Better ideas come along anyway, and you start to accept that you'll get to them when the time is right. Because you're the only one who can speak your baby's language and understand its cries, you begin to develop an instinct for what matters and what is just amusing. You are the thing keeping this child alive, and you are the only one who can force yourself to look up and see where it is headed. The earlier shifts were mere preparations for the transformation of orienting with the creation you developed and trusting that you know best.

Next up? Despite your being the sole provider for its incubation, your business baby will respond to outside influences, economic events, and—horrors!—things out of your control. It is hard to conceptualize because so much of your input equals its output (perspective check: the original goal for doing this), yet you do have to let it learn to crawl and interact with the world. Your once yours-and-yours-alone creation learns independence from the moment you welcome it, and the goal is actual independence from you. It will be hard to imagine putting this thing down, but it will get heavy and ultimately be an extra limb to carry. It's profound how that cord of extension can grow to be so large, and it's sometimes hard to define separation between you and the business now that it's out in the world. Understanding what the business needs will feel very close, very real; and it will become a priority. It will also feel like even your best efforts may not fix all problems or protect it from the bumps of life, which is hard to accept after the nurturing or preventative work you've put in to shelter it and make it successful. Even if you're prepared for the small stuff (i.e., the list stuff), guess what: life's lessons never show up when they're on a list.

Mirror, mirror. This cautionary tale comes as no surprise, but perhaps the depths of how much it matters to you will. You go along, nurturing this thing that feels amazing to cuddle and *Application to Business* love up. Since your baby is an extension of you, there is even more reason to remember to nurture the life that's fueling this machine—you. Even when your every instinct wants you to throw all of your energy at your beautiful creation, you must take time for yourself. *Make time for yourself.* Even though your connection makes you feel like the business can one day fulfill your every need (and you rationalize giving it your everything), it absolutely *cannot.* Just as much as you'd like to think inputs equal rewards, all entrepreneurs come to learn at some point that the ratio defies rational calculus. Sure, this is exactly why you took the risk in the first place, to see bigger rewards relative to your input. But there are plenty of times when there is not a direct relationship because once you're live, you can't control external influences. All the swaying and bouncing you do to keep your baby happy taxes your muscles. While its needs are 100 percent your needs, there is a point where you physically can't give any more. Remember that while there are short-term rewards of seeing your baby into the world, if you haven't taken care of yourself, who then is the business serving (that truly understands those rewards)? When you're busy nurturing this external baby and the externalities it's absorbing, don't forget there's also a beautiful child within you that still exists, even if this business doesn't.

And after all of this work, don't forget to have that launch party. Even if you only have a few subscribers or your business is entirely virtual, do celebrate the work you've done to get to this incredible place.

Expecting: The Delivery

▶ You'll know when it's time. Your baby will know when it's ready. You'll still survive if you time the launch sooner or later, but there will be a natural force that urges you to just do.

▶ Steal the time to stand back and stare at your creation.

☐ Your Readiness Journal

In these exquisite and evolutionary moments, what is coming up for you? Is it happiness, fear, frustration that things aren't as you planned? Make note of them and decide what they can do for your goals for the next few months.

_____

_____

_____

_____

_____

_____

_____

Slowing down to reflect on your goals is one of the hardest things to do. Getting by seems so much more prudent. But the composition of experience and the feels you came for can really become apparent if you're in the habit of this simple exercise.

8

And Then Baby Wanted Different Things

Expect Defenses

I loved being in love with my business. I loved being able to respond to its needs and help it feel loved. When things were going well, the peace and comfort from the relationship were real. I belonged and the business belonged, demanding moments and all. But amidst the care for your business, it is easy to get lost in caring for all the customers who also care for the business. There is a shift that happens often in relationships where couples go along, enjoying the rewards of their hard work in the relationship, but if one feels imbalanced, difficult moments can be polarizing. Suddenly the thing that you love intensely can catapult you to extreme frustration because you are used to feeling emotions at such extremes. When it's easy to flip this switch, you're in the e-paradox I mentioned earlier. You can easily go from loving to resenting the thing you thought you wanted to have. Resentment and likely other thoughts that come up are actually defenses and are here to help you tune into the dynamic of quite literally all the feels. Defenses of this nature or otherwise come on quickly, so be aware of how many people you're trying to please who are also linked to having your baby thrive. Feedback is as diverse as the number of contacts you have, which is a good thing if you're getting a vast array of feedback because that means you have a wide variety of customers.

Real-Life Example

My friend with the T-shirt company had a customer give her a hard time about a very specific element of a design that sold very well in her primary geography. Her product hadn't had a lot of exposure to customer feedback, because most buyers knew what they were getting before they bought it, via word of mouth, seeing it on a friend, or in a pop-up marketplace. My friend made an effort to collect feedback and had focus groups to truly vet her designs before launching a new offering, and the consensus was solidly positive. But one customer tried hard to convince my friend to change a bestselling design to better represent her personal interests, even going so far as to suggest my friend was catering only to more affluent clientele. This really rattled my friend. The feedback was from only one person, but it affected her psyche because she had gone to the effort to get a lot of buy-in. The dissonance was enough to take her mind offline for what would have been a productive two days while she decided how much she cared about the feedback, why it was bothering her so much to have an unsatisfied customer, and what she was going to do about it. She did not have extra funds to invest in a redesign of the shirt, and it certainly wasn't on her goals list for the year. I reminded her that it was a compliment that the person cared enough to write in and thought she was a big enough brand to incorporate every bit of feedback. I also encouraged her to do what was needed so the customer felt heard but to add the idea to the list of possible development.

Feedback can be hard to receive. It is especially difficult in the digital age, for the receiver at least; it's quite simple for the person dishing it behind the veil of a username. There will be tons of parenting advice, lots of it unsolicited. All parents experience it, be it of business or human experience. Unlike with biological offspring, you won't get angry emails from strangers talking about the choice of outfit you dressed your baby in (let's hope). But you will get some missiles from customers about putting almond milk on your menu because of the havoc it wreaks on the environment. Additionally, while feedback might be what makes *you* stronger, it might not be what the business needs to help it grow, so try to keep a healthy distance from feedback when you're still so closely attached to your baby business. Before I learned to have some perspective I had my staff check the Yelp reviews because, like my T-shirt company colleague, zinger feedback would invariably derail me anytime someone didn't like the thing I was pouring my every ounce into. Even when I could eventually look at it as data and opportunities to grow, it still stung.

Ways to Put Distance Between You and Feedback, Both Good and Bad

- ▶ Ground yourself before reading any written feedback.
- ▶ Accept you have no control over another's thoughts or actions.
- ▶ Change your perspective: feedback can't hurt you (unless you assist it) but rather it can always help you, even when you choose not to incorporate—it's always going to help (so be grateful).

▶ Plan to take action or make peace; do not read the feedback if it's not the time to implement change (if the feedback is helpful). If it's not relevant, commit to letting it go as not a match for your business.

Just do it well. The truth is that unless your business is solely based on volume, you can focus on quality over quantity. In other words, you don't need a lot of users, just a few good ones you can count on for good feedback. If you have a chance to really get to know a sampling of your customers, that is the best way to let feedback direct you rather than chasing everyone's wishes. It's widely said that divergent companies don't last, because if your product or service is confusing or overcomplicated, you risk losing the identity that customers expect when relating to your product or service. It's easy for consumers to rule you out, and in the digital age, to keep swiping. As long as you're doing your core offering well and not worrying about diversifying too broadly too quickly or after every suggestion, you should be sane enough to know when it's time to try on a new layer. The baby business bottom line is that you can't possibly please everyone, so aim for pleasing customers whom you either trust a great deal or who have said the same thing three different ways (by three different people). Your business and level of exposure will dictate how quickly your skin will thicken and how fast you advance this perspective. It's a healthy habit to regularly survey your customers to help with their engagement, your development, and the routine thickening of skin. Ideally you get to interact with them and ask them a very specific question on how you approached a problem or to get general feedback on some of your growth ideas. Do you get feedback for every move or pivot? Nope. Feedback, like parenting advice, can come from many directions and with varying degrees of interest of implementation. Sometimes it's solicited, by asking your customer how their experience has been thus far; other times, it comes in the form of a sour Yelp review from someone who caught you in a tough moment with new trainees or while preoccupied with some other solutioning. The important thing to remember—and hold true to yourself—is that you are in control of the direction you take your baby business. Sometimes feedback may require you to make changes on the fly, but your natural instincts and gut feelings are going to be what drives your business style. Be proud of the decisions you make, welcome some ideas from treasured customers to positively transform you, but recognize pleasing everyone will mean that you're operating in a transactional model and working for someone else.

Expect Growth Indicators

Accepting that not all paths are meant for you and being okay with the experience of choosing the best one is liberating. It's a tough pill in those early months, considering if this or that campaign/strategy/ advice will actually work, but things that work for some might not for others. An example from the real baby world is when my friend insisted we buy wipe warmers for our firstborn. It felt like this was in the "nice to have'"category and so we skipped the advice and instead used the money on a three-month supply of wipes. My son and his cleaned-at-room-temperature bum didn't know the difference. On a business level, some biz moms convinced me to buy a bunch of expensive National Sanitation Foundation (NSF) food displays to the tune of about $100.00 a pop, because if it is related to food, it's supposed to be NSF. These things were ugly, took up a lot of counter space, and reminded me of boobs. Besides, I prewrapped anything that was displayed and didn't feel so good about having to comply with "ugly" in my gorgeous tea shop. And because they were so pricey, I resented them even more. I wish I had researched how other cafes were getting past the health safety inspectors on this topic. I wish I had not been so hasty, because when I tried to sell the "boobs" on Craigslist, I found I couldn't even give them away. I wish my baby had spoken up, but who am I kidding, this was simply another lesson in figuring it out and earning badges of learning what *this* baby needed.

There was no way of knowing at the time of purchase that I would grow to dislike something that was raved about by people I trusted. Perhaps if I had been more connected to the needs, I may have tabled the purchase in exchange for something else. I may have found a way simply by refusing the status quo. Further, I use the anecdote as an example that you or the baby's preferences will evolve whether you encourage it or not. And you will quickly learn about agility and detachment from what you thought was important. As soon as you get comfortable, something will change, a growth spurt will occur. While it might feel like the evolution is dizzying, one way to manage it, to make it still feel like the business you've nurtured, is to regularly return to the beginning. Moms track an infant's growth via pictures and milestones. You can track yours against basic metrics on where you were this time last month, last quarter, or last year. Or you can look back at your goals three months ago and see what you've done, to ground you and embrace the accomplishments. Returning to the goals will also help you realize that you can still achieve, even if it looks a little—or a lot—different. While getting the baby to sleep through the night didn't happen the way you thought, you are getting into a routine now, and the future can seem clearer for having accomplished the milestone, despite doing it with a different method. The point is, centering on the goal (which usually doesn't change) can keep you from losing your balance.

Application to Business

Reflect, reflect, reflect. Returning to your summary of intentions (in some languages know as goals) monthly can give your baby the concentrated love it deserves and needs to grow. It will dictate your energy agenda, not your to-do list. Protect this time. In a perfect world, this exercise supersedes any meetings scheduled that day, and allows for only time to reflect and strategize. Besides punctuating what will feel like blurred months and even quarters, setting aside recurring time at the end of each month to evaluate any new internal or external threats or vulnerabilities and celebrate the successes or strengths will be fruitful. Let this reflection dictate your next month's goals based on how far you got or the results of the prior month's goals. You'll feel rooted and powerful, and even if the result wasn't what you hoped, you'll likely feel energized about devoting the time or effort into making it happen the following month. Not to mention the whole notion of staying close to your baby's evolution. Similarly, return to your business plan quarterly and protect time (at least a day) to be creative. Invite more specific creative planning in for next quarter by assessing where healthy goals may take you in three months' time, and take a snapshot of how you're trending.

Not sure what kind of goals to set? Well, look at the obvious ones (what's already on your to-do list, getting a bigger customer funnel, sharing more articles, getting into a good rhythm with managing finances, etc.) and be creative. Think about what's easy and then push yourself a little. If your goal is to have more one-on-one meetings with vendors so you can broaden your referral network this month, bump your efforts exponentially. If your strategic goal for the year is to get a thousand likes or follows, make sure you're doing something each month that ties into your quarterly and yearly goals. When you're the boss, it's easy to set unrealistic goals and then forgive yourself for missing them. One of the perks, after all, is no reporting structure! But in the way that getting dressed each day when you have a real newborn can be a goal (and some days may even be a stretch goal), remember when setting your monthly goals that they will drive your daily activities. While the boss *can* sleep in, if you don't give some thought to the upcoming month, your progress could get snoozed away if you don't have some motivating projects to keep you on track. If your progress gets stymied, it becomes way too easy to feel overwhelmed and then let your inbox or the low-hanging fruit dictate your day. Being strategic in your monthly, weekly, and daily goals will help you feel more connected to the cause and driven by the good vibes and smiles your baby business is eager to send your way.

Expect Experimentation

A friend of mine who owned a bakery gave me some invaluable advice when I was putting my menu together. She made suggestions where I should be able to use nearly every type of ingredient at least twice and set my pricing such that if I opened a package of, say, salmon, I could offset the cost of that one slab of salmon if only one person ordered a portion before the whole slab went bad. To this end, I only included ingredients that would stay fresh until I could order again. While that did make sense, I didn't know how many people would order from my food selections. Or how quickly I'd need to reorder. I didn't even want to have food initially but realized that if customers would be spending an hour or more in my shop, they would want some nibbles. So I crafted a basic menu and felt better about overlapping ingredients to make a shipment go further and the supply chain sound. It would be easy on the remaining operations and would not need too many updates to the POS system. There weren't too many ingredients to track, nor too much diversity of product to overwhelm the employees. And while I mostly achieved success in following her tips, the truth was that some weeks I could make it to the next scheduled delivery, and some weeks I couldn't. So early on, trips to the nearby grocery store ensued and had me reevaluating margins and alternatives on a regular basis. I thought I was in an okay place managing this way but vowed I would one day create a business that was the solution to small business logistic (storage and delivery minimums) and supply chain woes. Unfortunately, the problem compounded itself when my simple menu of fifteen items only lasted about three months because people wanted more. I resisted suggestions for different sandwiches; the menu was east-meets-west, to continue a theme of the experience the tea shop was selling. Eventually, though, I gave in to the staff suggestion for heavier options with rice bowls. I'd resisted due to supply chain challenges (extra ingredients to buy, track, and store) but getting the staff to create tea-infused dressings for the bowls was exciting to see and led to them creating soups with tea, a lovely new attraction that kept customers curious. It brought something so incredible that the pain of the supply chain seemed inconsequential relative to the awesome collaboration and freedom from controlling the supply chain so tightly.

Being open to the possibilities for change that the business is asking for can lead to helpful expansion after months of necessary bootstrapping. Sampling is your friend, and you get to learn through validation of sales or increased interest if it's worth the deviation from the plan or worth the extra steps. If you do have staff, having them own the steps to an idea they envisioned can pay dividends. Customers loved the rice bowls, even though they were pretty basic. The sauces made the difference and the staff were excited to be a part of that, something I would never have known had I not been open to a trial run. Their engagement helped grow the business more than a few cost savings surrounding the supply chain.

Crossroads and calculated risks. Will all intersections clearly indicate which is the correct turn? Nope. Is there a technique to help *Application* you know better? Not exactly. Knowing how to evolve will be *to Business* part of your story and what you get to learn about yourself. No business book will write the script for you on how to evolve, but some feedback and positive analysis against your goals can be the indicator that it's time to shed rigidity because it's no longer serving you or your business. Molting skin will feel right. Eventually. If something new is not

---

No business book will write the script for you on how to evolve, but some feedback and positive analysis against your goals can be the indicator that it's time to shed rigidity.

$ Goals

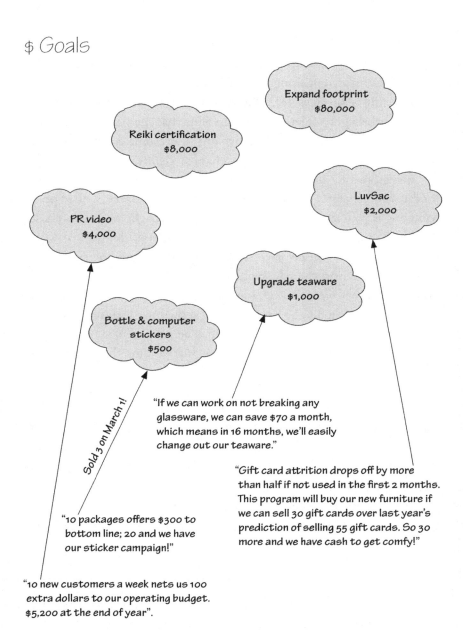

Expand footprint
$80,000

Reiki certification
$8,000

LuvSac
$2,000

PR video
$4,000

Upgrade teaware
$1,000

Bottle & computer stickers
$500

Sold 3 on March 1!

"If we can work on not breaking any glassware, we can save $70 a month, which means in 16 months, we'll easily change out our teaware."

"Gift card attrition drops off by more than half if not used in the first 2 months. This program will buy our new furniture if we can sell 30 gift cards over last year's prediction of selling 55 gift cards. So 30 more and we have cash to get comfy!"

"10 packages offers $300 to bottom line; 20 and we have our sticker campaign!"

"10 new customers a week nets us 100 extra dollars to our operating budget. $5,200 at the end of year".

Staff ideas to make it happen

working, you can always evaluate if the known, previous methodology is better than the unknown possibilities, or if a middle ground can be an alternative.

Even though it's hard work, you'll still be pleased with your decision.

Expecting: Learning about your Baby

▶ Codependency can lead to e-paradox and possibly defenses about some deeper feelings about the business. Separating you from your business means . . . it will grow up, so recognize areas for growth as just that.
▶ Stay close to your business plan, in spite of new ideas or ways it would like to evolve.
▶ Strategically revisit goals so you're evolving but not in a way you don't recognize your baby.
▶ Accepting that your baby knows a few things is good stuff..

☐ Your Readiness Journal

What you're expecting is important. It propels you and is usually in alignment with your goals and/ or your perceived satisfaction. Think about some alternatives to your short-term goals and what that might feel like or what new actions could come about. Comparing those alternatives to your original expectations, how differently has the outcome served your business?

_____

_____

_____

_____

_____

_____

_____

How do you feel now about softening to the unknown? Does it open up your curiosity or motivate you to attach more strongly to the goals of the business? Either scenario is right for the combination of you and this business you're nurturing.

9

Hiring Help

Expect ROI

There are two types of business moms: those who say they can (and want) to do it all; and those who see help as the quickest way to avoid having to eat their own offspring. Said differently, necessity may push a mom to rely on the help of others because their business model or the amount of time they're able to commit to it justifies trusting the care and feeding to someone else. Hiring my tea house employees and massage therapists was a business imperative; I absolutely needed to trust the brand to someone else while I was busy figuring out the business. To further illustrate the supply chain challenges, I tried to source our very limited menu from vendors who would deliver, but due to minimum-spend thresholds, I would have to order five times what I needed for the week to get the cups or produce that I needed. I tried a lot of other sources, but the trade-off to not having to store warehouse-style products in my tiny shop was either to purchase higher per unit from internet sources (and manage many more suppliers for each of my offerings), or go purchase it myself, which is what I did. I knew the pricing and available minimum quantities of the two restaurant warehouses in the area. For specialty items, I would procure from a gourmet delivery (with a $200 minimum) and source the rest from the grocery store. Being an early startup, those margins were huge and really affected our cash flow. In the beginning I was doing this myself because I couldn't easily transfer the knowledge I had, nor was it a good use of someone else's time to send them out to serve as our buyer. I'd personally rather pay someone else to handle the customers while I focused on cost savings and making those decisions as needed. Plus, I reasoned, think of all of the money I was saving doing it myself! But that meant even more time away from the store, and more backlog of CFO work or engaging with the customer on a potential event or other activities that included decisions at the highest organization level. So even though I had already hired, I came to a threshold of needing to hire more of the skills that were extensions of me. It was a hard transition, but recognize that there comes a time in every new mom's journey when you start to evaluate your days. That despite how much you love spending time with or getting smiles from your sweet little one, you realize you need a break in the to-do list. For me, it was easiest to recognize that the touch points with the events people could easily be done by someone on staff with the proper training. I wanted some involvement with the bookkeeping, but I didn't have to be the sole owner of it, so those were two easy ways to hire outside care for my baby. Some moms recognize their brain cells need a change and a challenge from solving the same problems routinely, and need to make time or space to innovate. For many mompreneurs, the reasons are different but the feeling is always the same: I've got to do differently. The good news is that if this business is right for you and you're making some money, you might be in a position to hire some childcare to watch over your babe while you go do the things you need to do or are capable of achieving. The hurdle is envisioning how on earth someone who isn't you will love your baby as much as you do? Well, no one, in fact, will be as deeply committed and spiritually connected to the business as you are. But letting go is a natural part of motherhood, as is trusting that a few select others will guide your baby when you can't.

First and foremost, consider if you can afford the help. Sometimes efficiency and automation of processes (via free technologies like Google Forms, integrations among software, or canned responses) can cut down on the number of tasks you'd otherwise hire for. Often, though, you can't afford *not* to get help because the time or energy you create will allow you to make more money for the business. You'll recognize you're at the tipping point when you simply cannot achieve the results without some shift in your focus, and yet the other stuff still needs help. While hiring is scary, you can always start small by offering only a few hours, or by a contract or freelance before committing to an official relationship. You'll know quickly if you need this investment and you'll get to look past your earlier fears of someone else caring for your baby.

Analysis. The decision process of considering what you will lose by way of cost and what you will gain should produce an *Application to Business* analysis that you will continue to use. It's about trust, and you can go nuts trying to analyze the trust factor. "Trust, but verify" is a mantra someone shared with me early on, and I was able to rely on that when quieting extra noise in my decisions to outsource the care of my new baby business. I knew I could justify the cost for the right person, which made the mantra work because I would be following up with references. If you do hire, consider a few factors when deciding if the worker could be classified as a contractor (passing the burden of tax withholding to them) or an employee (which means you get to tell them what you want and offer feedback, but you have to handle the payroll parts, or better yet, hire a service to do it for a nominal fee).

First and foremost, it's knowing the difference between an employee and a contractor. Reference the IRS 20 Factors. While it's pretty attractive to call an employee a contractor to avoid all the taxes and laws associated with having employees, most arrangements are defined as employment (like reporting to work at certain times, being told what to do or how to do it, wearing uniforms, etc.), so understand the difference and choose carefully. A few things to note on becoming an employer:

If the business pays an independent contractor more than $600 in a year, the business is required to report this using IRS Form 1099. A business is not required to withhold or pay employer taxes payments to an independent contractor.

Employers are responsible for

▶ Tax withholding (FICA)
▶ Unemployment insurance
▶ Workers compensation insurance
▶ Reporting withheld wages (I recommend using a payroll service and thus, the fees should be in your projections—usually a per pay period fee plus a few dollars per head, and worth every penny to calculate, withhold, and file the monthly and quarterly taxes for you.)
▶ Employment eligibility (Immigration Reform and Control Act 1986) and verification
▶ Staying in compliance with other employment laws (such as Americans with Disabilities Act).
▶ Understanding union requirements and any right-to-work laws (which prohibit union shop or closed shop and cannot deny a person the right to work on account of membership or nonmembership in a labor union or organization). These vary state by state.

- ▶ Understanding state labor regulations (minimum wage, equal pay, child labor, apprenticeship training, and bulletin board poster requirements).
- ▶ For more info, contact the Department of Labor.

It seems daunting, but being able to contribute to the economy (and that translates to properly administering the tax programs) is something that will help you feel proud and validated, not to mention relieved for the quality help.

Expect Trust Discovery

Despite war stories you may have heard (the old negativity bias is everywhere; brains retain—and share with you—more negative info than positive), you can still find loyal workers who want to see you succeed. Mark Zuckerberg says you should hire someone you're comfortable working for. (He also says they should be maniacally determined.) I can't disagree with that. My mom liked to hire people who needed the job the most because they often worked hardest. I would add if that person was also qualified and would enthusiastically take something meaningful off my plate, their interest helped me feel good about their work ethic if I knew they were personally motivated to serve in the role.

When setting my intention on who to hire, people who brought qualities like intelligence or aptitude, self-motivation, goal-orientation, likability, and comfortable communication always ended up being staff who stayed with me the longest. There will be plenty of times when you hope people can read your mind moving at rapid speed, but they can't, so being comfortable having conversations (when you're too tired and fussy yourself) will be key to sustaining a trusting caregiver relationship. Here's another great place to get feedback from folks in your industry or area who are a little more seasoned. No two people are the same, so you can't take anyone's advice verbatim unless you're hiring the same person under nearly exact circumstances.

Primer on When to Hire

First, determine that you absolutely need to hire. It's a big expense. Question if you simply need a better system (CRM like Hubspot or Highrise) to streamline things, or if your pain points necessitate a whole person. You'll know pretty quickly if your list of things you can't or don't want to do spans beyond existing tools, but it's always worth a pause. Similarly, consider how other lean startups would solve for this problem. Some businesses wait until the operations can fund before hiring. Recognizing not all business models can function this way (retail or restaurants, for instance), it's worth considering if you truly can start small.

First, you'll need a job description that screams your company's values and uses words that describe you as a person, because you *are* your company and you should have no concerns presenting that way. But remember, this is a job description, so it needs to be impeccably clear. You need X to achieve goal Y and in Z way. Weed out applicants based on what you have written, which should reflect your mission. Figure out before you interview what characteristics you need to hire out (someone who is organized because you're not; someone who can manage their own time because you can't help with that; someone who can teach you about coding while they're also your assistant . . . consider doing a strengths assessment and figure out what really matters to *you* in this investment). Remember: make no concessions at the screening stage. There will be plenty of times when you need to when working together, because people can have personal emergencies or undesirable tendencies.

When it's time to interview, these important questions will help you get to a deeper level and explore your comfort with them:

- ▶ What brought you to apply for this role? What were you looking for?
- ▶ What about our site or job posting speaks to you? (*You'll get information about them as a person; let those details lead to a few more probing questions about their character and preferences.*)
- ▶ What is your brand? (*intentionally open-ended question*)
- ▶ What makes you tick? How do you like to work?
- ▶ What makes you happy? Inside of work and outside of work?
- ▶ If resources weren't limited, how would you live life?
- ▶ What do you like most about your current job?
- ▶ What are you most proud of in your career so far?
- ▶ If you could use all of your strengths and contribute in a meaningful way, what would you be doing?
- ▶ Among your weaknesses, what can you see yourself overcoming and how?
- ▶ What are you bringing to this position and what do you expect to receive in exchange?

So many people asked how I found such great talent. I first say that it was merely good fortune, but it's also about being true to my framework for hiring. Even friends who applied to work with me were required to use the standard application via my website because the questions tied back to the *why* of the business. I also looked for someone who could carry an interview because it showed they were poised, interested in possibilities, proactive, and could function on my behalf, serving customers to secure the future of the business. I always ended with a question that aligned with the character of the business: We sell an experience that's surrounded by relaxation. How would you say this matches your innate skills or value offering? This may seem like a tough inquiry for a retail job, but it set the tone on what they could expect and how much of their authentic selves I needed since I was taking the time to make sure the fit was matched across many levels.

Application to Business

Core strength. It is an exercise in trust and hoping for the best because you simply don't have a crystal ball. When you can take the leap, as in most things, the net appears and it all works out. Either the person adds value and frees you up for great things, or it's a mis-hire, in which case you're one step closer to knowing exactly what you need and you'll be much more prepared next time. The second goal of the CEO job description, but arguably of equal importance is also to keep the money coming in so they stay in your employ, for the record.

Hiring people who can figure out what to do and how to do it is the first hurdle, then once they're here you still have to regularly and consistently engage them. Give them ownership decisions (this may be hard when it's a brainchild), but letting them make suggestions on inventory, processes, or protocols will help them feel more connected to their work and the vision . . . and hopefully be motivated by the trust you place in them. It can be so liberating and invigorating to watch someone blossom into an employee you can trust. And that you trusted yourself to see through the possibilities of expanding your company.

Expect Effort (Employee Engagement)

What does an entrepreneur who quit their job too early do with extra time on their hands? Write training manuals and employee handbooks! There are companies who will do this for you (like payroll companies or startup consultants), but I say you should do it yourself if your time allows; it is so much better to be intimate with the content than going

When it's time to bring on staff, your main goal as CEO is to set the tone and bring people who can execute the vision. Simple as that.

around trying to remember what you read. And even if your manual is only half documented, make sure to give your staff good training, even if you're still figuring out processes. Entrepreneurs are comfortable navigating ambiguity, but not all people are. Type A checklisters prefer structure, and their own value can be tied up in a job well done, so make sure you're giving them the tools to be successful. Complete employee manuals and training documents for a small startup were well received by new joiners. To have such a thoughtful onboarding experience helped embed them in the culture, not only in the interview but also in follow-through to their first formal weeks with me and the company. Those materials did certainly evolve as I learned what the business really needed or as new systems were brought on or more streamlined approaches were developed by my incredibly loving staff. Plenty of CEOs prioritize other things, like sales, before manuals, and I get it—you need to have the cash to pay for the staff. But the sooner you bridge "how" via the manual to your why, the sooner you're inviting yourself to scale the business. In creating manuals, you're creating the possible. If not for creating a path to train someone, then hopefully for reduced turnover thanks to the deeper impression they'll have of you and the company you're running. What values should you instill? I had to ask myself what makes a good employee or contractor and think about what they were doing to be high functioning and top notch. What steps were they taking to make it perfect? Not that perfectionism was my goal, but exceeding customer expectations meant we all had jobs, and exceeding my expectations meant I could focus on other things. So I wrote it all down in very detailed fashion and explained why it mattered. I had regular newsletters to the team (*TEAm*) from day one (on payday) whereby I let them know what they needed to know to be successful: new promotions coming up, how we were doing financially, specific knowledge about certain herbs, teas, or service offerings, and a personal note of gratitude. This reinforced the care I had for the team. Even if they didn't read it (some did not), they put a little more of themselves into the job because I did, by setting a strong example (their words, not mine!). They also stuck around because that increased love they found in themselves to share helped them intertwine with the mission a little more tightly.

Whether it be detail spelled out in a manual to help them feel safe, or taking the time to teach them via written or verbal communication, a staff person will stay longer because you took the time and you showed care. They will try harder and they can even align more closely with your mission if your materials are interwoven with the mission as well. Some of my longest-standing employees contributed and imparted their gifts and fingerprints into the business. They knew I helped them get started, but they quickly learned I wasn't perfect and in reality knew nothing about coffee (being the tea lady and all) or cooking. They saw gaps, took it upon themselves to add to the training curriculum, and helped smooth orientation for the next hire. Be prepared to be humbled by what they may add to your startup because they're proud to help grow your baby, too.

Application to Business

Engagement is everything. You can build trust and hire the best employee, but like everything, it's the follow-through or how you maintain the relationship that counts. Sure, there will be a few mis-hires or employees who aren't ready to show up the way you need them, and that will be alright, too. Clear expectations and alignment with the *why* in the job description, interview, and manual can help the least experienced person further along in their journey. If you've done everything you can to meet a trainee where they are and there is still a gap, you can look to either aptitude or training. Sometimes it's worth a look to see if your materials need to be refreshed (usually once a year, or as new processes are implemented). You can learn all about the miracle of keeping employees engaged and satisfied in book 2: *Ready: What to Really Expect When Raising a Business*, due in 2020.

Expect the Fog to Lift

Some articles urge a new entrepreneur to bootstrap everything but splurge on a few important things like a nice chair or a high end CRM. As a girl who defined bootstrapping by shredding grocery bags to make gift basket stuffing to save the $4.99 price at the store, a nice chair for my tush is not anywhere close to the priority list. But sanity that I could get it done if I had a little help was at the top of that list. Besides, my hiney wasn't sitting but instead was all kinds of hustling. One expense I had zero hesitation on however, was investing in a payroll service. There's a lot of talk about minimum wage increases, and unless you've worked in a HR-related role, you may not know a lot about taxes or implications of having employees over contractors (and what types of work contractors are allowed to do if they're not an employee). If you can afford it, it's best to hire a payroll company that will stay current with rates and calculate everything for you; there are many online tools that do it very economically. This was one of the best investments I made, because my payroll specialist explained everything and made sure I was in compliance and handled all the changing tax rates and monthly, quarterly, and year-end filings on my behalf. With this off my plate, I could focus more on how much payroll was costing relative to revenue instead of calculating tax rates and complying with filing deadlines.

Streamlining this easily outsourced function is smart, but if you choose to use a contractor or cut the checks yourself, it's still worth reviewing the IRS website on employees versus contractors and even getting advice from an accountant. Salaries can easily be the biggest expense of a business, and that has a major impact on your overall revenue and income position. Payroll companies will get the money to the staff, but you still need to be familiar with laws being passed that affect your position as an employer (like minimum wage, health care, etc.).

Application to Business *It's worth it when you can afford it.* Most times, employees are exactly the sunbeams that cause the fog to lift, and hiring someone is a very big deal and worth celebrating. This may seem like a far distance away, but it's not as far as you think. It will happen before you know it, and then you get to reinvent yourself and how you spend your time now that you've made space for your own greatness!

Expecting: Growth through Hiring

▶ When seeking data for timing your own hiring, do seek advice from parents-to-be in your industry about when they knew it was time.
▶ With thoughtful training come thoughtful employees.
▶ This is a big deal, so plan to invest in a payroll company to share some of the regulatory burden. You can enjoy the pleasures of sharing your workload, not just creating more work by trying to be a bookkeeper or stay on top of tax filings and withholdings.

Your Readiness Journal

What makes a good employee for you? What are their characteristics and abilities? Even if you're not ready to hire today, think about what a future addition could bring to your company.

_____

_____

_____

_____

_____

_____

Now that you have envisioned a person, create a task list of what that intern, personal assistant, or sales associate would be doing. Next, what would you be doing with that extra time?

_____

_____

_____

_____

_____

_____

10

Priorities and Sustainability

Expect Leveling Up

When the baby sleeps, you sleep, right? Well, this isn't exactly an analogy that follows the business birthing experience, but it can apply in the sense that when the business is resting on its own, your arms can be free to not be productive for a sweet minute. This "sleep time" can look like a to-do list that is 50 percent complete (it will never be done), getting into a rhythm with your tasks, or some perspective that those tasks are just tasks and there's no need to balloon their importance. It's a healthy place to be! While your baby is resting, take advantage of these moments to keep your wits about you. Even if the baby is not resting, your sanity may need you to set the baby down and walk into another room for a few minutes. Some days I had to take a lap around the block when it got too heavy; some days, I took five minutes to nurture me, even in the vein of business in some proactive healing space I had created. One of the first things I did when I felt the slightest bit of rhythm to my business was start to seek out expertise on trends or areas that were relevant to me. I didn't do this with all of my free time, but I certainly did it when I could. This way, I felt the impostor syndrome a lot less and believed I was stealing away some luxury time of my choosing without completely wasting it reading magazines that did nothing for my goals. I remember seeing old partners I worked with reading the *Wall Street Journal* and thinking "what a life!" but I then realized it was a necessity, not only for their abilities but also their sanity.

Doing things for you in the early days may seem self-indulgent, because the baby business does need a lot of your energy. But thinking about what you can do that serves you as a whole person, and not solely a mom to this business, can ease you into doing what helps you feel empowered and healthier. Eventually you *will* be stepping away in the name of sanity and you *will* be in the habit of taking mini breaks in the name of *you* that will feel like a graduation or an arrival and less like a programmed guilt trip.

Application to Business   *Stay relevant.* Some things to do with your free time while baby is entertained in the bouncer include

- ▶ staying on top of trends for marketing or industry trade by frequenting hubspot.com or mashable.com's focus on social media. Other fields have curated news based on their industry (such as Publishers Marketplace for publishing).
- ▶ reading inc.com or entrepreneur.com because they speak to small business in ways that don't intimidate you or make you feel small next to the moguls.
- ▶ reading *Forbes* or allthingsdigital.com, which is the *Wall Street Journal*'s overview site on technology. Let's face it, technology

is not only synonymous with success, it can break you if you don't embrace it.

► setting and resetting achievable goals that get you to the next goal (not ever busy work/doing all the time) and reflecting on what you're working on/consumed with now and how it will matter years from now.

► setting intention words (i.e. expand, ignite, purpose-led, heart-driven, magnetic or transcendent) about your business and how you're serving a real problem in your customers' worlds.

► taking time to think big after the words to describe it have been established.

► recognizing that when you're powering through is when you most need to take a break.

These are all great to level up and help keep your confidence bar high, but please don't forget that there is also a need to disconnect from everything, including the need to think bigger. *Even my better self agrees with this.* Remember the goal to spend 10 percent of your time recharging your own batteries and reconnecting to your own power source, whatever that is. If 10 percent of your week is this other kind of self-care, let 2–3 percent be the brain care that keeps your mind from turning on itself. You need it. It needs you. While this exercise might help your foray into true disconnection for sustainability, it is the technique that will rejuvenate a heart-centered business mom. If batteries need it, you better believe that humans need it in spades.

The goal to spend 10 percent of your time recharging your own batteries and reconnecting to your own power source, whatever that is.

Expect Baby Steps

When you start to feel like you have the hang of things, it is precisely the time to carry on as though *you do not*. I made the mistake of assuming flow would continue and got very attached to filling out my 10 percent buffer with enhanced podcasting, regular lunching, and being on top of my to-do list when the fog of newborn life lifted and I started to feel like a human again. But no surprise here: all things in moderation. The more I layered on in terms of work I could be doing to be a smarter, better version of myself, the more attached I was to working that way, such that when a new challenge arose or I lost a little agency over my time, I had a bit of resistance to letting go of a few of my new habits.

A better choice would have been layering in each new habit (one TED Talk per day for a month, then layer in reading certain articles between tasks/shifting mental gears the next month), so it wasn't such an adjustment when all I could afford was the usual work, the current challenge, and maybe just one of my new habits per day. As in life, entrepreneurs know the next wave is coming and they need to orient themselves whenever they can. But those waves are still worth the work. The highs and lows of business ownership are the trip that you set out to enjoy. The composition of experience and all its detail makes it both vivid and distracting at the same time.

Application to Business

Stress signals. Staying on your game is a joke when you're a one-woman band. The tempo will change, you will fall out of rhythm, and it will feel like the wheels are coming off or that you will never have your stuff together. Recall that listening is the number one but hardest skill for entrepreneurs, and it's mostly listening to yourself. Listening isn't even the hardest part: honoring the message is. If you're feeling stressed, it's important to own that and recognize that stress decreases empathy (and let's face it, all we really have is relationships). Chronic stress is tied to memory loss, brain fog, and loss of self-control. So take the time to go to your doctors' appointments (both metaphoric and real), and take the time to play, because your brain cannot be depressed while you're playing. Prioritize space-creating because your ability to generate power is directly proportional to your ability to relax. Fanatical is a word common with successful founders (ideas born of passion and personal desire to fix something) but fanaticism can take over your personal mission. If you're not properly fed, you can't properly take care of your baby. Create space, even if it's only making a monthly appointment with yourself and establishing routines to support your postpartum health.

Expect Healthy Detachment

By now you might have asked some entrepreneurs what their advice for being a success would be. Many told me there is no such thing as success in the short term. If I had to answer the question based on my experience, I'd say success is accepting the marathon, no matter which mile you're on. I heard someone call their first ten years in business their "overnight success," and since then I have observed that ten years is about the time it takes for a business to really take off. That's ten years of responding to your business child's needs. That's ten years of hard work. Keep that in mind when managing your own expectations. Other regular check-ins are how you're doing against your own expectations; you can do this by taking a dedicated weekly mom day to ask if you're doing the right things for your life and your role. Actively choosing releases dopamine. These pauses are different from the monthly disconnect to realign with your business goals. These are regular touchpoints on how you're spending your time. An accountability partner might do this for you, but if not, make a date with you and your list to be intentional about what you want and what the business needs. I would choose fifteen minutes at the start of the week to assess goals, since the end of the week was usually crazier trying to wrap things up. These Monday minutes were my time to set the pace and choose business and personal goals. Even if the week didn't allow for it, I felt better for having set out to protect the time, and it became an even bigger priority the following week. It is how I managed each mile in the race.

Choosing things to clear your head or contribute to your energy reserves isn't selfish; it's serving your business. Similar to putting your own oxygen mask on first, you are going to need space to recognize when decisions are not helping your goals or you. Powering through is not always proven to be successful, so recognize when you're doing it, and set your intention on doing it differently. Never has sprinting for miles on end worked for humans, so take that time. I was so conditioned to power through that in that first year I was willing to take on things that meant a lot of work and not a lot of return. I made changes to the website that never served the mission because I didn't think about what those enhancements meant . . . or didn't think about how much time it took away from doing purpose-driven work. If you can't take a full day to clear your mind and reset your priorities, try to do a check-in at the end of each day. If I had set my intention at the beginning of the week, I found these check-ins much more spiritual and found much more gratitude for the work I was doing, even the mundane or the tests. If you can find daily breaks for meditation or general care, the check-ins may not be needed as much.

Not sure what to do when you're taking time for yourself? Here are a few ideas.

▶ Walking meditation (10% Happier app has plenty of guided meditations)
▶ Something that moves both your arms and legs at the same time helps the heart rate and the common plague of home-based-entrepreneur lassitude
▶ Anything that you cannot put on a list

▶ Volunteering is wonderful and cathartic but unfortunately can sometimes become another thing on the list, so choose your time meaningfully

---

If you got hung up on something or went down a rabbit hole, set your intention on love, clarity, connectedness, awareness (of whatever caused confusion or distance from the goal) and wait. Even though you may have left flow for a moment, you still are doing your dharma and can bring yourself right back to good by connecting with the soul of your business through a loving mantra or prayer for your beautiful growing baby. You are in fact connected to your business, and your body can tell you the answer if you allow it the space, check-ins, or general examination that you and your baby business deserve.

Nature. Believe it or not, this is the beginning of the baby becoming independent. The child always learns to assert its independence, and the parent always rails a bit but then eventually enjoys some newfound freedom. The baby business may take on a life of its own, but ultimately your nurturing values are a part of its identity. You get to figure out that dance in the years ahead. Many times, the founder's syndrome becomes a beautiful threat: you believe you are ready to distance yourself, but the company only knows how to exist with you at the top. The baby thinks it wants to grow (for sustainability and longevity), but the truth is it doesn't know a vision that isn't in tandem with you, so don't panic if you still have the need to be needed. With your care, it will learn to feed itself, crawl, walk, and eventually find a way to survive on its own. But in the meantime, you get to learn what's best for each moment, and the centrifugal force of the dance that rewards you and keeps you spinning will take on shapes you may not have anticipated or appreciated. And even deeper rewards than you dreamed. The next chapters of a business life are no more surprising than the early months. They too will serve to awaken you, and as long as you've endured the first year or two, you have the lifeforce and the stamina to navigate the rest. And we'll be here to mama sherpa you along in your journey.

Expecting: Postpartum Health

▶ At any point, whether with relationships or with business, you're either expanding or contracting. There is no such thing as maintenance mode. If you're flat today, you're likely shrinking tomorrow for not pipelining or infusing loving energy into the business.
▶ Habits matter! They create your experience and your business.
▶ The moments where you feel like this is the end need to be nurtured; it very well could be one of many waves. But be honest with yourself and be in the practice of coming up for air and nourishing yourself.

☐ Your Readiness Journal

When you're nourishing yourself you are . . .

_____

_____

_____

_____

_____

_____

_____

_____

Conclusion: What Got You Here *Genuinely* Helps You Get There

What will feed *your* success? That determination, perspective, and resilience you've honed through the birth process. That clear alignment with your yin-like nurturing side and knowing when it's time to turn on the yang. That knowing yourself, trusting your wisdom, and recognizing your plan can guide you more than you know because you put love into the process. Your success will look different with the changing weeks, but it will be success because you're doing your purpose and you're opening to the experience, lessons and all.

Everyone wants the best for their child, wants them to be happy and well versed, speak languages, get athletic or academic scholarships. And usually, life's "best" is exactly what your child gets for their growth, even if it isn't exactly as you envisioned or dreamed. The truth is, you have no idea what the future holds or how successful your baby will be, or even if it will all be worth it. But by and large, it is. Even if lots of money is lost, or you decide entrepreneurship is not for you, you've still gained. Even if the business does not prosper, you have, personally. You're doing more than a lot of people have found the strength or means to do, so be proud. My mom had a good ten years with her TV and appliance business before deciding the battle with the big box retail scene of the 2000s was not something her lease or location could sustain. She believed her fortitude could win, but ultimately she chose her sanity. It was an incredibly hard decision for her, but the writing was on the wall with trailing revenues and industry trends becoming more and more apparent. She honored the good years and decided to exit on a good note. She does miss the good days, but in her heart she knew the uphill battle would have meant more strife than happiness. I'm proud of her for being honest with herself and figuring out what was next for her after those dedicated years.

And that's the way entrepreneurship goes. It's glamorous in that you're being bold and learning a level of self-confidence you never knew you had, but sometimes there is flow and sometimes there is clamoring to figure out what the heck you're going to do next. Swings from high success and low panics can create emotional flips that make the success meter feel utterly broken. I assure you that when you look back on your journey, no matter what the bank account says, you'll recognize how much you've learned and how you've grown, but you'll also appreciate something special inside you. A better understanding of yourself will probably be the most pronounced. The mirrors a baby business puts in front of you teach you a lot about how to solve problems, but they also teach you about vulnerabilities or insecurities you might not have discovered if you hadn't put yourself in a new and sometimes scary position. Having a business is an exercise in getting comfortable with the uncomfortable. Getting comfortable pretending you have the answer until you trust yourself to make sound decisions for your enterprise, and welcoming lessons on patience, will come up until it's embedded in your personality. Getting comfortable with only so much being in your control despite the world telling you that you must be in control. These are all lessons that you may have to sacrifice money or time to learn, but trust it's worth it.

And resilience, oh the ways you'll learn resilience. Recognizing when you're on a roll means that change is coming, so the good times are the times to get ready. Still celebrate, but don't get carried away lest you be flatfooted. My friend has a successful app and still celebrates when a new brand name wants to partner, even though she's seen them come and go throughout her business life. Give a high-five and say hallelujah, because as soon as you think you've gotten your baby's diet figured out or their sleep routine in place, it will change. And relationships change, too. I spent a lot of time working out ingredients and pricing with a couple of exceptional, local natural product makers. We had great contracts and an exciting outlook. Except both of them (independently) moved out of the area for life reasons and dissolved their businesses. While not anticipated, this was an opportunity to meet other vendors, reuse my learning, shortcut some back and forth, and figure out a new path forward. Each change that comes may not be ideal, but one thing is for sure, you won't get bored. They're here to evolve you. If change and evolution seem a bit much when you're still figuring out what is (much less, what will be), consider reading *Who Moved My Cheese* to help you embrace the nimble nature that business will teach you.

As you look to the future and the constant evolution to stay current, relevant, or even connected to your business, you'll probably find yourself comparing your business to others, like moms tend to compare the size of their babies to similarly aged babies. The chubbiness, amount of hair, how much they're eating, sleeping, cooing. It's normal. It's not that we're *that* vain, but I betcha the third- and fourth-time moms are doing this way less. They have figured out that what matters is peace. They *know* that worrying won't help, it affects the milk supply, and by the second or third time, they realize their timing and effort will either collide or not, while all that looking around only detracts from the experience and risks feeling neurotic.

As you look to the future, your skepticism and critical eye for time and value become sharpened. I found myself asking daily if a particular task was driving revenue or funding my dream, even in the early days. But when you catch yourself in that space, it's a good moment to pat yourself on the back and realize you're becoming a more resilient business mom. It doesn't mean you're becoming too "business" but that you're getting smarter in your approach to having a loving, sustaining relationship with yourself and respect for your own output of energy, and the vision you have for your baby.

Broadly speaking, you get to look at yourself through the lens of creation. You get to be the farmer and the consumer. You get to see, touch, feel, learn, and understand which hat you're wearing at any given time. The role of business mom is all-encompassing. It's easy to get lost in the details, but the aim of this book is to help you practice pulling back from the devilish comfort of the weeds, to appreciate evolution in business, and to remember the "you" in this whole trip.

More specifically, moving from mundane responsibility such as having enough money/not quitting your job just yet, to exciting responsibility (having enough energy to do yet another job) means grounding in what you don't know lovingly by making the best decision for today. Do this by still considering the thrill of the near-term rewards with the mundanity of what's needed for the grown-up baby and then make peace with the decision that matters most to you, today. It is so easy to get lost in uncertainty when it's your first, but remember all that this business is asking of you: decisions that have an eye for the future but make sense for today. Remember that what we focus on grows stronger and that discontent can be loved because it evolves us.

Even when your life isn't being rewarded with baby smiles, you still have to nurture the relationships and keep going. So add personal care to your checklist. Even if it's only one website you have time to follow, let it be ours; we'll try to aggregate all the cool new options for startups that we come upon and mantras to help fuel you.

As a business mama, things you haven't even thought about will surface. Things like your staff unknowingly giving away supplier information, or new competition popping up once you finally figured out your market. It may feel like getting off the hamster wheel is impossible or improbable since it is your *dream* it is fueling. But get off the wheel you must, even if it's one of the harder things you'll do. Taking a vacation does require considerably more work, especially if you have a retail or ecommerce presence or don't have a sister-wife to look after things. Even if your business is truly transportable and you can take the whole thing with you on your trip, saying no to emails and customers is necessary. The future of space for your greatness is in your hands, as is the future of success. And do call for vacation, and do practice resting your soul so you can be more vivid and present in your working days. Do align with what makes you happy and light at heart; business can be a fast way to make the world around you seem so serious. Every mama needs a break and is usually a better mom for having taken the time. Birthing a business does not mean a life sentence or a short leash of endless responsibility, but it can be if you don't take breaks. And don't forget to leverage your power to raise an independent and successful offshoot of you.

If the spiritual/purpose anecdotes don't speak to you, perhaps the "when to quit your job" themes can help guidepost your journey to a business you feel good about bringing to life. As much as you'd like to move quickly through this process, time is your best friend, and with time you can learn to make strong decisions. And the more practice, the better you get at making them.

A practice of looking at yourself in the mirror and saying *you're doing it!* will evolve you more than you appreciate today. You will be proud you paused for a moment to acknowledge the pressure to get you to this point. The motivation came from somewhere, the determination was mustered from within, and the spirit to carry on can be found by looking at your purpose or at yourself in the eyes in the mirror. By doing this, you're creating an opportunity to really connect with your deeper self and your vehicle to actualizing your self-worth. Be proud, mama. You're doing what this lifetime has called for. You're taking risks and being true to your purpose. *It will not be easy.* No diamond is created without pressure. All the practices of tuning into your instincts as a mama throughout this book will hopefully allow you to be aware . . . to recognize there is no ease in evolution. Everyone, especially women, should own a business or become a parent in this lifetime. If done with an open heart and a curious mind, it can be the value-adding, perspective-seeking, sustainability-delivering experience that nature set you out to have.

Follow www.lyndseydepalma.com for more information, find downloadable resources mentioned here, and more to light up your startup journey.

Sneak Peek for Upcoming Books

Ready: What to Expect When Raising a Business

The story goes on for another five years. More beautiful surprises and some hard pills to swallow. The roller coaster of thrills and chills and incredible people continues. The hard realities around staffing, supply chain, and maintenance of a retail space do create challenges that aren't easily solved in a perspective or mindfulness exercise. But solutions do evolve and deeper love for the business that created me (not the other way around) can be noted. In this next book, I go into detail around how startup lessons take a new shape. I introduce tools and tricks that I came upon as my baby business became a bit more independent, and I tell you what that meant for mama as the business began scaling.

Ready: What to Expect When Moving On from Business Creations

If you googled me today, you'd see that I eventually sold my sweet tea shop and had to get a lot of coaching along the way. The finale in *Ready: What to Expect* is again a mix of how-to but also holy-cow-didn't-see-that-coming experiences. As taught in business school, you have to start at the end (the exit) before you can really build a business. This exit was not the one I imagined, but it was one that brought all the personal and business lessons, just like starting it. Ultimately the new owners will go on to close the location they acquired from me, but with plans to try again in another state in the hope that the legacy lives on.

Appendices

Appendix 1: Advice for a Full Business Plan

A long-form plan will cover a lot of the bases if your business will require traditional funding or getting a professional comfortable working with you. Here is what to include.

- ▶ **Cover letter**
- ▶ **Cover sheet**
- ▶ **Table of contents**
- ▶ **Executive summary:** This is usually created at the end, but for purposes of organization, we introduce it here, where it serves to help keep your reader engaged with the big questions answered up front, to temper the newer questions that start formulating as you get into the crux of the plan.

- ▶ **The opportunity:** what problem your business is solving and what unique attribute you're offering. This is also where you can put your mission statement, which is meant to be a reminder to customers and employees of why the business exists.

- ▶ **The business:** how you're organized (legal entity), how you'll make money, what you'll do with it, when you'll break even, and what your cash flow situation is for the first two years as laid out in budget projections (income statement, balance sheet, cash flow analysis, and capital expenditures). Depending on the age of your business (if you're rereading this at a later time when it's time to seek big girl funding), the balance sheets and other pro forma reports are often irrelevant since in the beginning, you're making your best estimate. We will get into the nitty gritty, but detailed business plans usually also have the key business ratios (again once established) and explanation of financing needs/anticipated use of funds.

- ▶ **Marketing:** how you'll reach customers and the total analysis of industry and competition. Here's also a good place to really define your mission: it can help you be more specific as you think about the ways you can attract revenue. You can also drill down into your product or service description, proprietary nature, and any competitive threats in this section. Wrap up with the overall marketing strategy, pricing policies, selling distribution channels, and servicing methods.

- ▶ **Financial:** how much it will cost to reach customers and how much you'll (ideally) make when you do. To thoroughly prepare, you have to do your research. Really looking at what's involved can be done by looking at how much it's going to cost. The purpose of this tedious exercise is to decide if it's all worth it when you think about how much is on the line.

- ▶ **Management:** the players who will bring the business to life. These are officers, current and ideal org charts, responsibilities, and even resumes of key personnel and composition of board of directors/advisors (if you're taking this business plan for multiseries funding, for example).

Executive summary of the business plan: this easily can be taken to banks and initial meetings with real estate agents or vendors to whom you're not ready to reveal the full plan. The executive summary should include:

Management team	Business description
Industry	Company background
Number of employees	Management experience
Bank	Technologies, special know-how
Auditor	Market/distribution channels
Law firm	Competition
Amount of financing sought	
Current investors	
Use of funds	
Financial projections for 5 years (revenue and EBITA)	

It shouldn't take much time to do this, and it allows you to hold your cards a little closer to your chest while keeping the interest of someone who may not have time to read through your whole plan.

Appendix 2: Advice for Creating a Pitch Deck

Recall the storytelling skills discussed in your elevator pitch? Leverage those same skills to tee up a formal pitch to potential investors. If you're lucky enough to be going big, or even thinking big, a pitch deck is worth the effort to put together alongside your business plan. The order of the business plan elements can be used to set the order of your deck, however if you're going for the big money and are delivering this pitch to investors, they'll also want to see:

▶ Five years with revenue and EBITDA (earnings before interest, tax, depreciation, amortization)

- ▶ VC firms want to see a path to $50M in revenue
- ▶ How you'll monetize and scale the business
- ▶ Current status on this trajectory
- ▶ Road mapping and where you'll go in short term (and how fast you get to good)
- ▶ Funds requested and use of proceeds (VCs like to see sales and marketing as use of proceeds)

They don't like to see back pay, legal fees, excess R&D, based on feedback from several VCs. Be prepared to speak on the business plan components and addressing the points above for fifteen to twenty minutes. While not needed for the slides, you should be prepared for some general questions outside of the presentation, such as

- ▶ What advisors are you working with (especially in small towns or when a lot of money is requested)?
- ▶ What is your acquisition strategy?
- ▶ What partnerships (realty, talent, or vendors) do you have making you/your idea relevant?
- ▶ What research supports that data?
- ▶ Can you think of a better market this could work in? *(trick question, I think)*
- ▶ Have you thought about changing your name? *(although a legit question, if they're thinking about ways to capitalize on their investment, it's an easy way to get thrown off your pitch game)*

My best advice: Do several trial runs in front of your friends and business colleagues who can ask the critical questions and fully prepare you for the difficult questions and shark-infested waters of delivering a pitch. Other advice that I have stumbled upon from investors:

- ▶ Never say "the percentage of market that needs to be captured." Say the why, what, and how of it being captured, using active voice.

▶ Never say these numbers are conservative. While it might be attractive to have that be the baseline of returns, an investor wants you hungry and saving your conservation for expenses (and not revenue). If asked about the numbers, you can say they're vetted.

▶ Speak loudly. If you're naturally a soft talker, get someone on your leadership team to present for you. Confidence is the name of the game in this scenario, and while loud (aggressive) voices are not ideal in every business setting, they seem to be what the crowd needs in the pitch room.

Appendix 3: Advice for Parents Who Will Need a Retail/Commercial Space

If you can have a pop-up space or sublease to try it out before committing to a big investment, do that. If time involved equates to space a topic takes in this guide, the topic of space identification/negotiation/implementation would deserve its own book. There are lots of pieces, and this is one huge step where a lot happens on someone else's timeline. The good news is that the process can be started early and can be happening in the background while other things are being sorted out. The other good news is that it should get easier with the second child, when lots of your needs are already sorted out, so you go in early asking for all that you realized were sticking points when the first lease was all said and done.

Once you have a general comfort with how much you can afford rent-wise, you'll need to quickly test the market and make sure you're not too off in your projections. It's a little hairy as to which comes first: get a real estate agent to help you figure it out, or get your best estimate at what you can afford and then approach the broker. In my experience, it was the former, and every real estate agent I met with wanted a bulletproof business plan with sound projections before they'd take me on as a client or allow me to bid on a space. Bankers will also want your bulletproof plan before they will consider a loan and grant you a commitment letter. Trouble is, your business plan won't truly hold water until you have real numbers to test and validate the model. So your best bet is to do as much research as you can, interview a few commercial brokers for general rental rates (including triple net: taxes, insurance, and common area maintenance) and use these numbers to determine how many square feet and in which location you can afford. Unlike residential real estate, which is published on any real estate agent's website, the CoStar (database that houses commercial listings) is strictly limited to the brokers who pay the expensive dues to see listings. So doing research on your own may be tricky. My local county-sponsored BizLaunch team did have access to the CoStar reports, so I could see what was available before reaching out to a broker, however I didn't figure this out until two absentee brokers later. Another place to look is loop.com which does have some commercial listings, but the information doesn't appear to be as realistic or as up to date as it could be. Unless you are hoping to hang a shingle in a town where there aren't a lot of real estate options, simply approaching the leasing agent or landlord usually doesn't fly because typically the landlords enlist agents to seek out specific types of tenants, and less common is a renter who stumbles upon them by chance.

Whichever way you gain access to a list of what's available, try to do this early enough in the process so that if you need to change locations or direction, you'll still have flexibility in your time budget as well as your brand scheme. Interview real estate agents early on and make sure you're comfortable with your representative (see interviewing skills in chapters 2 and 9). Next, solidify your preferred zip code, and pull data on the demographics (the landlord should have median income and related statistics) to finalize your business plan before talking to the banks. The minute you have an interest in a location (before the LOI is even inked) be sure to first navigate your jurisdiction's regulatory environment. Zoning regulates the location of uses, including different types of businesses, and generally needs to approve the business use by certificate of occupancy (this is sometimes lumped into a total special use permit).

Understand the timing around these aspects. I had looked at a near-perfect space in the town next door and was about to proceed with lease documents when I found out only one person reviews all permits and I had one chance to submit it the right way otherwise it would be rejected and I would need to wait for the next review month to submit again. It happened to be nearing summer, and the approval boards took the summer off, so the soonest I could get approved for my use would be four months from then. It broke my heart, but I had to walk away. Something similar happened with a beautiful space that required an elevator and that the ADA bathrooms both be on the ground floor, essentially rendering all the expensive real estate I would be renting out of the picture for revenue generation. Even though you do your early due diligence with the context of your business (understanding what is required—occupation licenses and fees, for instance, before you can even apply), there still exists the risk of heartbreak as you get attached to a space; and there is of course, still the aspect of timing. In my jurisdiction, zoning took seven weeks to approve the initial plans and seven minutes to approve the certificate of occupancy (CO). I'm told it can take anywhere from four to six weeks to get a CO, based on the type of work you're doing. When I applied for my CO for Home-Based Business, I got it in twenty minutes after waiting in line at the county offices. This information is usually available in the jurisdiction's website, or someone can look up the exact address if you have it in mind at the zoning office. Even internet businesses must have a home occupation certificate.

Before signing a lease, be sure to go to the county zoning office to review any site plans for the location you're hoping to lease. If it's a sophisticated/planned area, be sure you review any documents that might lay out what the landlord and county previously agreed to use the space for. In my instance, I had to amend a Retail Attraction Marketing Plan (RAMP) before I would ever be granted a CO. This process would have taken up to four weeks had I waited until it was time to open to realize that my CO would never have been granted because the specific use of my business was not laid out in the RAMP. This very thing happened to my sister in the same county, and her landlord was not helpful, because hers was a large real estate conglomerate who did not allow her to negotiate the point that rent would start immediately, whereas my landlord agreed to charge rent only when construction was done, and they even helped me amend the RAMP for specific use of my space. The timing of permitting is relevant even if you're doing nothing to a space but hanging a sign (there are usually multiple permits for that: electrical, mechanical, structural). There are so many facets of understanding a business's zoning requirements, but hopefully you have access to a BizLaunch within your jurisdiction to help you navigate.

Understand what other licenses/requirements might be needed in order to operate in your jurisdiction. The conversation with the zoning commissioner helped me learn that in order to get a CO—the final step in opening—I first needed to have my food license, reflexology certification, food safety plan, detailed description of my menu (which was subject to change regularly) and how each item would be sourced and stored (within food compliance), recycling plan, construction permit (timing) for all alterations other than painting. Good thing I had nearly six months from the time I signed the lease till opening to work these out. The jurisdiction states that it can take fifteen to sixty days depending on jurisdiction. What it doesn't say is that many (*many*) underlying inspections happen leading up to that point and at any time, you can fail an inspection and then be required to halt other layers of construction before you can proceed or they can come back. This is where the timeline really becomes null and void.

If you're dealing with a buildout, it becomes even more complicated. BizLaunch was able to put me in touch not only with the appropriate building inspectors to get answers straight from the horse's mouth but also the ADA specialist and the sign and health department commissioners, to help me understand early on what challenges my use may encounter from their respective viewpoints. There are many interpretations in a well-organized jurisdiction, and you may get the runaround from well-intended associates who interpret the details in a way that is less than helpful. This happened when I went to speak with someone about my signs. Admittedly, the regulations had recently changed, but I went back three different times for different questions and the responses were different each time. I finally had the last woman write her opinion on a sticky, and I kept it in my file for when the official came to tell me my sign was in violation. It was a verbal warning, but when I called the county to clarify once and for all, they told me the sign was fine and that everyone should be on the same page going forward. Best advice is to document every little thing when dealing with regulatory affairs. You can also hire a buildout contractor who knows your jurisdiction's requirements and who will own most of the permitting for you, if you negotiate for this. Trust that they have a better seat at this table than you.

When determining what you can afford, consider these in addition to zoning:

- ▶ cost of rent for space
- ▶ visibility
- ▶ image, parking for customers/employees, highway, street walk-in access, loading space, compatibility with nearby businesses. In many economies, rent should be a third of revenue.

Contrary to what most stakeholders want you to believe, a personal guarantee is in fact optional. Depending on your situation, some landlords (as well as lenders) may accept a statement from the bank verifying there are large enough assets such that the guarantee isn't necessary. If they want your loan in their portfolio, this is certainly negotiable. For my first lease, it was a ten-year term but we negotiated (among many other things) down to a two-year personal guarantee. In other words, as long as I paid my rent on time for the first two years, if I closed shop in the remaining eight years, I would not owe the rest of the lease term at the time of lease termination.

Ask to see exclusive clauses they have with other tenants early on, and be clear about your menu/goals for businesses. Despite having a discussion about using a panini press (you have to outline all of the intended equipment in the architect and construction drawings), I found out that another (not yet opened) tenant was a nationally recognized sandwich shop and they took offense to my offering a few tea sandwiches on the menu. While it wasn't in breach, it was certainly a surprising clause that crept up when the actual lease was drafted, and it resulted in my vowing that sandwich sales would never cross a certain threshold of sales.

As much as you don't want to deal with big name landlords because they likely won't be helpful to startups, they won't want to deal with you, either. They prefer the big credit, and besides, to them, startups are not only risky to waste time with, they can come with a lot of requests. Even my relatively small landlord was skeptical on how I would fund operations and scrutinized my projections because I only came with a house as collateral and not an existing brand or restaurant group to back my cash-flow assertions and ultimately my ability to pay rent. Fortunately, they liked my business idea and didn't have any better offers at the time, so they took a risk on me. Sophisticated leases should be in writing and outline exactly who is responsible for what when various types of incidents occur. A commercial lease should include

- ▶ how much rent and escalations, how long the lease runs, and specifically when it begins and ends and conditions for renewal.
- ▶ what, if any, utilities, parking spaces, amenities are included.
- ▶ maintenance expenses, property taxes, or insurance and how they'll be calculated.

- if a deposit is required and if a letter of credit can be used instead of cash (standard is asking for a two-month deposit, however *everything* is negotiable).
- sign requirements and allowances.
- a detailed listing of any improvements the landlord will make to the space before you move in (usually willing to do more the longer the lease term).
- restrictions the landlord will place on tenants as a result of your signing the lease (parking spaces, exclusives, etc.).
- assurances that the space is zoned appropriately for your type of business. (*This is not the landlord's role; they just want your money and commitment. It is you, my friend, who needs to confirm this.* My sister had to petition the zoning office after the build-out had commenced because she learned after the fact that her space wasn't zoned for a yoga studio, despite being recruited by the landlord.)
- whether subleasing is permissible and if so, under what conditions.
- how either party can terminate the lease and under which conditions.

These additional elements seem to show up in every sophisticated lease I've looked at:

- noncompete clause
- dispute resolution
- spatial specifications
- default termination
- additional costs
- build-outs
- sublease
- term options

Some landlords (and even your real estate agent) may try to rush the LOI process and encourage the negotiations to occur only when the lease is drafted. In my experience, landlords do not want to revisit terms that they felt should be put to rest because they advanced past the LOI stage. The LOI is critical from the tenant standpoint, as you will get a pretty standard lease and the landlord will not want to engage in extensive negotiations. So make sure to go over with your broker any other deal points that may be critical. Surprise negotiation elements for me included

- ▶ hours of operation (they cared when I would be closed, mostly)
- ▶ what is rent during option period
- ▶ potential cap on taxes and operating expenses passed on to you in first two years, especially if you're in a mixed-use situation
- ▶ ensuring the common area maintenance is specific to the commercial tenant and not something the residential tenants will be enjoying but not paying for (e.g., vacuuming and cleaning areas that are untouched by the businesses)

Here are a few more fun facts/tips about leases.

- ▶ Escalations are pretty standard (3 percent and most landlords won't budge on this because inflation will rise but their rents may not). One alternative is to keep the rent flat for five years and then a 15 percent bump rather than 3 percent per year to get the business off the ground.
- ▶ Tenant improvement allowances exist. Ask for as much as you can; this will certainly affect your cash flow in year one.
- ▶ Every negotiating point in the lease really is money. Savings here gets baked in there.
- ▶ Get receipts from contractors; make that a part of your contract. You'll need them when stuff starts breaking and the contractor with your money is long removed from your job.

- Get recommendations for contractors and anyone you will need to be working with for a long period of time.
- Plan to marry a handyperson; you'll need to call on someone monthly after the buildout has happened.

Appendix 4: Tools to Love

Check www.lyndseydepalma.com for more as we discover new tools to journey with.

CRM
- Hubspot, Highrise, Infusionsoft, 17Hats
- Ontraport (if you're big-time or have funding already) combo CRM/marketing source

Operations
- Adobe DocuSign, HelloSign

Storage/Collaboration
- Google Drive (or Box.com if you have a lot of AI-rich files)
- Asana, Slack

Marketing/Social Media
- Hubspot for all the education you can dream of on this topic
- Mailchimp (free for first 3,000 subscribers, then immediately pricey)
- Hootsuite (but check the Facebook limitations on reach before publishing)
- Ripl, Wordswag, Canva
- Unsplash for free images
- Boomtrain (if you can afford) to better work with machine learning to understand your readers and then populates newsletters to personally tailor to your individual customers

Finance

- ▶ QuickBooks online, Wave accounting (also has payroll), Shoeboxed
- ▶ Indinero (best if you're scaling quickly)
- ▶ FreshBooks for service-based companies
- ▶ Mint.com if you're not looking to invest in reports but rather a free way to track your spending/finances

Sourcing/Freelancers

- ▶ Upwork (quick solutions, perhaps not long term freelance relationship)
- ▶ Task Rabbit (contractor/handyman especially if you have a physical space)

Books/Similar Research/Resources

- ▶ NOLO
- ▶ Sheblogs: things I wish I knew before I started a business
- ▶ The Small Business Start-Up Kit: A step-by-step legal guide (NOLO) that includes how to price
- ▶ Onewomanshop.com/2015/100-best-sites-for-solopreneurs/
- ▶ Bushra Azhar's Persuasion Revolution podcast

Appendix 5: So What Did My MBA Actually Teach Me?

Overall it taught me situational navigation skills. Putting myself in the shoes of business executives as they navigated their ventures really helped me appreciate a perspective I might not have ever taken if I hadn't equipped myself. But as I look back, the lessons via case studies that were big enough to take away seemed to distill down into these themes:

1. Always hire a professional. Always.

Advice clearly for well-funded businesses, but when minimizing risk and being efficient (which applies to all business sizes), it's something that textbooks, case studies, and professors echoed. However, as a startup, bootstrapping may not afford you the luxury of getting an attorney to draw up all of your contracts, although there are certain things that you simply can't skimp on. Unless you are an accountant opening your own accounting firm, get the help of a professional at least to get you on a path and budget as best you can in your startup expenses. It's so much cheaper in the long run. Always hire a lawyer, and make sure your projections account for legal fees. Here's a great question to ask some local mentors you attach yourself to. *Which professionals did you bring on board and at what stage did you make that investment?* Most everyone will likely say don't try to lawyer on your own, and I would agree if you find the ones who like small business. They are pricey but worth every penny.

2. Best-laid plans mainly applies to system design

Most MBA classes won't teach you how to write a business plan, but you'll study many and will know the outcome of those that laid a good foundation and ones that didn't. A business plan won't make your business, but it will certainly help you plan appropriately and set you off in the right direction. After the plan is written, you won't present it at every initial meeting you have, so most businesses then create a one-page summary (called an executive summary) to offer before sitting down and talking feasibility with anyone.

But the planning that really matters is how the business will function. These are at the mercy of reality and will change regularly. This was taught in lecture and validated in real life. See *allll* the anecdotes presented here, aspiring parent, *and have a backup plan.* Especially from a logistics and resource perspective. If your best-laid plans and reorder points still leave you without hotdogs in your stand, the pickle isn't so much that you ran out but that you didn't have a backup plan. Supply chain is one class I would encourage the budding entrepreneur to take. Or at least study up a few scenarios online to really appreciate how business can be impacted (shipping/lost sales) when proper planning isn't carried out. If your business is more service oriented, you'll still need to play out how your systems talk to each other, and while there was a class for it, my main takeaways are there are a lot more inputs to a business than I appreciated, and you really have to think through what they are. And of course, as represented by the industry, there are lots of different requirements for any business. Unless you can afford an enterprise tool, you'll be piecemealing your CRM with your accounting software (because one will have limitations and usually can't serve all the needs of each individual business customer). So give it your best . . . and take the class only if you're already comfortable with your business elements and can put them to test among the other types of businesses that design systems to support their processes.

3. Everything is money, especially growth

I'll let you know how much that is in the next book about business rearing. You cannot grow your business without significant investment in marketing, employees, or infrastructure, and this costs more money than most businesses appreciate and is where they find themselves in treacherous waters. Growth is expensive. *Bottom line*. So plan for it.

4. Unmanaged cash flow will kill a business

In most scenarios, a safe estimate is six months' worth of expenses in your projections. Depending on the amount of in/out flows, the amount you should have in your bank account should cover three months' worth of all of your fixed expenses. This was pretty consistent across most businesses that we studied (from small to medium size, that were successful past their first two years). Sure, an affordability perspective is available by checking the cash reserves, but without thinking hard about how that money might already be committed (subscriptions to tools, payroll, or fixed costs), it's really difficult to know how much investment you can safely afford in your earlier years, as so much can shift in a day. My best advice is to also take the approach of *let's assume there is zero in the bank at the time of the decision.*

How much more money do I need to earn to afford this? If I needed to hire a general manager, that meant I needed to make X more dollars a day to cover their salary, plus what I needed to keep in the business or service loans with, plus what I needed to take home. If I wanted to participate with the expensive Yelp ads, I needed to see ten more customers a day to afford it. Everything was carefully rationalized . . . okay, scrutinized. It helped my cash flow tremendously.

5. Most businesses fail, but no one expects it to be theirs

The MBA entrepreneurship track teaches you this through numerous case studies. And staggering data suggests that it's at least 80 percent of businesses that fail, with recent studies suggesting the number is closer to 90 percent. The verdict is still out on how close these ratios hold true. My entrepreneurship professor worked with fifty startups in the DC area. Forty-nine are no longer in business (although some of them made a lot of money before they took a tricky turn). Odds are yours will face a few trials that will test your model, but even Harvard MBAs have companies that have failed, so decide how much of a risk you're willing to take for the sweet rewards called entrepreneurship. You're probably already a risk taker by nature if you're still into your plan and reading this. And if you aren't in the very small percentage of businesses that survive, you'll have a wealth of knowledge to apply to your next startup (which tended to be the case with most of the businesses we studied).

6. Always have an exit strategy

Whether it be that you'll sell your company to a larger name or pass it down within the family, you will need a way to leave the business healthy. Dissolving the business is not an attractive exit strategy. Having an exit strategy not only keeps a light at the end of the tunnel for you in dim times, but it shows that you've thought through everything and that you see this entity as a viable offering or service that may be better led by the next wave of CEOs than not. A note on strategy in general: Look at things like variables and attributes and it will make more sense. Map out causes and influences. Sometimes the strategy is to stay right where you are, but knowing your options and deciding one way or another is the difference between controlling your business and the alternative.

7. Scaling, especially globally, still comes back to culture

Even in emerging markets (we visited Chile and Argentina), successful commerce still had everything to do with local elements. A hardware store with a dominant presence in the United States won't last in a community where the successful businesses are investing in the community, sourcing resources locally, and yielding to cultural customs and not imposing US-based standards on employees. Sure, this is one example, but the message rang true: You can't expand into new cultures without relating to the new customer and culture the same as you would in your US-based marketing analysis.

8. Marketing matters

Specifically, differentiation and first mover, pricing satisfaction, and value satisfaction. Know your demographic. Know where they shop, what they do with their free time, and use research. Don't make assumptions—they're expensive. The MBA teaches you how to apply statistics to marketing and calculating the ROI, but as a startup, you can do all the research and build plans and simple calculations to the net impact. Save the MBA marketing tricks for when your company's valuation is coming in at the multimillion level.

9. There is no right answer

This was the best lesson of all: It's about how you navigate. This gave me the confidence to start a business despite the things I didn't know that I didn't know and quickly learned. The businesses we studied took different approaches to challenges. Some worked for them based on their circumstances, though it might not have been a decision that worked for all the players in the market at the time. I would say that the confidence I gained was worth the MBA. But can folks find the confidence without a business degree to increase their threshold for pain? Totally. My sister had a career in sales. She had a huge commercial conglomerate for a landlord, and she was able to navigate those treacherous waters, but her confidence was different from mine. In her early days, even though "no" not being in her vernacular helped her deal with tricky landlord situations (that had me in hives hearing about), general business scares would have her reacting in a much more pronounced way. Full disclosure: She had a much bigger space and a much larger loan and personal guarantee riding on the line, so her short-range perspective was justified. But the big message here is that in time, and as I write this she's moving into year six, she most certainly learned the ebbs and flows of business and is a lot more comfortable with the tides that inevitably change.

Works Cited/Resources

Allen, David. *Getting Things Done: The Art of Stress-Free Productivity.* Piatkus Books, 2019.

Agrawal, Miki. *Do Cool Sh*t: Quit Your Day Job, Start Your Own Business and Live Happily Ever After.* HarperBusiness, 2015..

Breus, Michael. *The Power of When: Learn the Best Time to Do Everything.* Vermilion, 2016.

Engelhart, Matthew, and Terces Engelhart. *Sacred Commerce: Business as a Path of Awakening.* North Atlantic Books, 2008.

Gerber, Michael E. *The E-Myth: Why Most Businesses Don't Work and What to Do about It.* HarperCollins, 2012.

Gerber, Michael E. *The E-Myth Revisited: Why Most Small Businesses Don't Work and What to Do about It.* HarperCollins e-Books, 2017.

Ingebretsen, Mark. *Why Companies Fail: The 10 Big Reasons Businesses Crumble, and How to Keep Yours Strong and Solid.* Crown Business, 2003.

Johnson, Spencer. *Who Moved My Cheese?* Vermilion, 2002.

Kashdan, Todd. "What Do Scientists Know About Finding a Purpose in Life?" *Psychology Today*. February 24, 2015. www.psychologytoday.com/us/blog/curious/201502/what-do-scientists-know-about-finding-purpose-in-life

Kim, W. Chan, and Renée Mauborgne . *Blue Ocean Strategy: How to Create Uncontested Market Space and Make the Competition Irrelevant*. Harvard Business Review Press, 2016.

Kramer, Marc. "7 Factors That Get Angel Investors to Write a Check." Bizjournals.com, The Business Journals, 7 Feb. 2015. www.bizjournals.com/bizjournals/how-to/funding/2015/02/7-factors-to-get-angel-investors-to-write-a-check.html.

Osnabrugge, Mark van, and Robert J. Robinson. *Angel Investing: Matching Start-Up Funds with Start-Up Companies*. Jossey-Bass, 2000.

Raz, Guy, et al. "How I Built This with Guy Raz." NPR, 20 Nov. 2017. www.npr.org/2018/01/02/562899429/ben-jerrys-ben-cohen-and-jerry-greenfield.

Schultz, Howard, and Dori Jones Yang. *Pour Your Heart into It: How Starbucks Built a Company One Cup at a Time*. Hachette, 2014.

Sincero, Jen. *You Are a Badass at Making Money: Master the Mindset of Wealth*. John Murray Learning, 2018.

Nhâ t Ha nh, Thích. *No Mud, No Lotus: The Art of Transforming Suffering*. Aleph Book Company, 2017.

TED. *Start With Why—How Great Leaders Inspire Action*. www.youtube.com/watch?v=u4ZoJKF_VuA

Vaynerchuk, Gary. *The Thank You Economy*. Harper Business, 2011.

Acknowledgments

My deepest gratitude to all my comrades in the journey to entrepreneurship: the trip has been and continues to be memorable and incredible. To everyone who offered advice, shared stories, were a part of the journey, and lit up my path, I am forever in your debt. There are entirely too many people to point to with all the goodness that networking, synchronicity, and opening my heart brought to me, but this list has and continues to have a direct impact on my entrepreneurial experience.

To Mom, your example of determination and having fun even when the days were hard has set the mold. Employees and customers alike have commented on how passionate I am on the subject, and I know it's all from you.

To Dad, my saying I couldn't have done it without you is an unjust understatement. You stepped in when I was recovering from delivering back-to-back human babies, from washing bottles to linens for the tea shop, and were a sounding board when the times got trickier than this new mom was mentally prepared for. I didn't even have to ask, you just sensed and served as village leader in immeasurable ways.

To Amanda, my sister, who was the first I pitched the idea to and the one who was by my side through funding seminars to fall outs of tough negotiations. You are the epitome of tenaciousness and kindness balanced beautifully, and I'm proud to be related to all that, proud that your baby Mind Your Body Oasis continues to thrive, and forever proud to call you my sister.

To Cynthia, the sun and moon of my MBA program and dear friend and ecommerce, technical systems, and user experience expert. You had my back, gave me so much confidence and even more creative design work (in conjunction with John!) that I am eternally grateful for you and your perspective on business and life. I'll drive you across America any day.

To my fellow entrepreneurs who were also accountability partners, creative problem solvers, or space holders when I needed to unload or get unstuck: Lisa, Shana, Jeff, Sten, Patty, Alison, Megan, Alex, Carolina, Carriebeth, Kirsten, Nicolette, Claire (and my mother-in-law, Evelyn, who introduced me to the dynamo Claire), Debijo, Jake, and Pleasance, you all truly made a mark on my experience. I found inspiration in every. single. conversation we had and believe I wouldn't have found my way if it weren't for your examples, reassurances, or clutch advice.

To my grandmas, who have all made a huge impression on me: Arletta the late-in-life entrepreneur, Agnes (deceased) the herbalist, Isabel (deceased) the writer, these ladies plus my mom have gifted me with not just my feminine strengths but also have laid the foundation for how we do and aspire to do in this life. These women have made a significant mark in the detailing of this story.

To Kristen and Karen, my beta readers, your advice, generosity of time, and advice have been humbling and just lovely.

To Joey, my friend and the guy who *actually* got this book to the finish line, you simply rule.

To Melissa Lew, designer extraordinaire and friend to the end, your ideas and passion to create are inspiring.

To Dick Margulis for your keen eye, creative talents, and your ability to keep me honest, I am so grateful to have found you.

To Lauren Taylor Shute Editorial and team, you brought what would have been a book about an agonizing business timeline to life. You were my doula to this manuscript and allowed me to enjoy the process. I'm particularly grateful to Lauren for the sage business perspectives and fun conversations we have shared through this journey. There have been numerous professionals from her team involved with this book and to each of you: you. are. magical.

And to Nick, the voice in the back of my head, the guy who really taught me about perspective (and negotiations) and the one who has endured *the most* lessons in patience as I follow all the paths this righteous life has offered, you are remarkable.

About the Author

Lyndsey Clutteur DePalma is a mindful business sherpa, helping business leaders make decisions that are strategic and purposeful, resulting in companies that are sustainable, high-impact, and fueled by love and intention. Drawing on her experience as a retail business owner, consultancy founder, and business coach and mentor, her passion is helping entrepreneurs and companies realize their potential and have fun fulfilling their purpose.

DePalma integrates all of her experiences, including being a mother of two and of-service to many, to foster a perspective that not only honors the person in the driver's seat but also the person they're becoming as a result of the work that's in front of them.

Made in the USA
Las Vegas, NV
26 April 2021

22062955R00157